LOCAL AREA NETWORKS:
Selection Guidelines

INFORMATION SYSTEMS & NETWORKS CORPORATION

James S. Fritz
Charles F. Kaldenbach
Louis M. Progar

PRENTICE-HALL, INC., Englewood Cliffs, New Jersey 07632

Library of Congress Cataloging in Publication Data

Fritz, James S.
  Local area networks.

  Includes index.
  1. Local area networks (Computer networks)—Purchasing.
I. Kaldenbach, Charles F. II. Progar, Louis M.
III. Information Systems & Networks Corporation.
IV. Title.
TK5105.7.F75 1985   001.64′404   84-9929
ISBN 0-13-539552-6

Editorial/production supervision and
  interior design: *Lynn Frankel*
Cover design: *Photo Plus Art (Celine A. Brandes)*
Manufacturing buyer: *Gordon Osbourne*

© 1985 by Prentice-Hall, Inc., Englewood Cliffs, New Jersey 07632

All rights reserved. No part of this book
may be reproduced, in any form or by any means,
without permission in writing from the publisher.

Printed in the United States of America

10 9 8 7 6 5 4 3 2 1

ISBN 0-13-539552-6 01

Prentice-Hall International, Inc., *London*
Prentice-Hall of Australia Pty. Limited, *Sydney*
Editora Prentice-Hall do Brasil, Ltda., *Rio de Janeiro*
Prentice-Hall Canada Inc., *Toronto*
Prentice-Hall of India Private Limited, *New Delhi*
Prentice-Hall of Japan, Inc., *Tokyo*
Prentice-Hall of Southeast Asia Pte. Ltd., *Singapore*
Whitehall Books Limited, *Wellington, New Zealand*

Contents

PREFACE — v

1 INTRODUCTION — 1

2 THE EVOLUTION OF LOCAL AREA NETWORKS — 3

Contemporary Local Area Networks 4
Network Topologies 7
Control and Access 11
Transmission Mediums 13
Network Architecture and Communication Standards 16

3 MODEL APPROACH TO LOCAL AREA NETWORK DESIGN — 19

Technical Approach 20

4 DETERMINING LOCAL AREA NETWORK REQUIREMENTS — 25

Required Services 25
Network Traffic 31
Reliability 36
Growth Requirements 37
Network Administration 38

5 ALTERNATIVE TECHNOLOGIES   42

Private Branch Exchange 42
Baseband 46
Broadband 50
Hybrid 54

6 COMPARISON OF ALTERNATIVES   56

Evaluation Criteria 56
Life Cycle Cost Factors 57
Cost Analysis 58
Trade-off Analysis 64
Weighted Rating Comparison 71

7 CONCEPTUAL DESIGN   73

Physical Network 73
Message Network 76
Control Network 82
Conclusion 85

A LOCAL AREA NETWORK SYSTEMS   86

B LIFE CYCLE COST FACTORS   93

C REDUNDANT EQUIPMENT RELIABILITY   96

D DATA ERRORS   98

E PACKET TRANSMISSION   101

INDEX   105

Preface

Local Area Networking is yet another successful combination of two distinct technologies (communications and computers) to create a significant advancement in the data processing industry.

Students, engineers, and managers anxious to learn about or take advantage of the benefits of Local Area Networks are often confused by the vast quantity of information available. There are hundreds of vendors on the market proclaiming the advantages of every type and combination of network topology, medium, control, and access.

This book provides a guide for both the lay person and the professional in the rather complicated process of selecting a Local Area Network. The text has been organized so that it is easily read and understood by the non-technical person, yet in specific areas it provides enough technical detail for the systems engineer. The volume provides step-by-step procedures to illustrate how alternative Local Area Networks can be selected for a specific facility, and it explains how these alternatives can be evaluated in terms of desired attributes. Examples are provided throughout the text.

Students will find in this book both a useful introduction to an increasingly important topic, and a text that offers a clear, organized overview of the technical disciplines involved.

Engineers and executives will find that the methodology demonstrated in the manual provides an exacting approach to the selection and evaluation of a Local Area Network. The procedure presented eliminates a subjective selection process already made confusing by the presence of a bewildering number of systems and vendors.

In addition to the authors, other Information Systems and Networks Corporation employees contributed to the development of this text. Richard D. Bakula, Barbara A. Judd, and Richard M. Martin deserve special mention for their efforts.

James Fritz
Charles Kaldenbach
Louis Progar

1

Introduction

Local Area Networks (LANs), although not a new technology, have recently seen many new applications and developments. Along with this has come the availability of a vast number of systems, which has made the selection of a specific LAN a rather complicated process. This book describes in detail how a LAN can be chosen for a specific facility, and how the available alternatives can be evaluated in terms of selected attributes.

The four major network systems discussed are private branch exchange (PBX), baseband, broadband, and hybrid. A theoretical facility is described, and each of the systems is then evaluated for this facility, using weighted criteria methodology. With this approach, you can easily follow through the selection process and then apply the same process to your own facility.

The text has been organized so that it can be read and understood without difficulty by the nontechnical manager or executive, yet in specific areas it goes into enough depth to satisfy even the most detail-oriented systems engineer.

This first chapter is purely introductory. Its purpose is to tell you what the book is all about, who should read it, and how it is organized so that you can get the most out of it.

Chapter 2 provides background and tutorial information for the executive who is considering the installation of a Local Area Network. It describes the components of a LAN and clarifies specific terminology used in the field. This material may be bypassed by the engineer who is already familiar with LAN operation.

Chapter 3 describes in nontechnical terms the model approach used to develop each of the alternative LAN designs. It basically provides an illustrative step-by-step method for determining network requirements and system design. The methodology is then used in the following chapters.

Chapter 4 discusses factors which should be considered in determining Local Area Network requirements, such as anticipated services, the types and amount of traffic expected to pass over the network, the degree of reliability required, the expected system growth, and the network management and control mechanisms that will be needed to properly administer the operation of the network. This chapter introduces our theoretical facility to give you an idea of the types of factors which must be taken into account in considering a LAN installation.

Chapter 5 presents simplified design layouts for the four alternative approaches to fulfilling the requirements discussed in Chapter 4: the PBX, baseband, broadband, and a hybrid of baseband and broadband. Although the descriptions are written for a systems engineer, they are presented in a logical manner for comprehension by a nontechnical manager. The chapter describes how each type of LAN can be adapted to our typical facility.

Chapter 6 proposes a method of evaluating the four alternative LAN designs to determine which would be the best for your own use. A weighted matrices technique is described which can be adapted to any situation. Again, our typical office is used to illustrate how the weighted matrix technique is employed.

Finally, Chapter 7 introduces a conceptual design of the Local Area Network selected in our example. Although one acceptable solution is derived in this chapter through the use of our model, this should not be construed as the only possible solution. Many possible solutions may be tested through the use of the model by performing the calculations with different input parameters. The detailed design in this chapter may be bypassed by the executive, but will be most informative for the design engineer.

The nontechnical model approach, examples, and weighted matrix evaluation process are the key to the utilization of this manual. The model is actually an illustrated step-by-step approach to be used by anyone desiring to select and develop a LAN system for a particular facility.

The charts provided can be applied to any number of installations for the purpose of determining requirements and costs, and for analysis. The weighted matrix can be adjusted on the basis of the user's criteria. If costs are not important and reliability is, then the weighted value can be adjusted accordingly. This methodology allows you to adopt a quantitative rather than subjective approach to the selection and evaluation of a LAN.

In summary, this manual will provide an illustrative step-by-step approach to a Local Area Network selection and evaluation process that can be used by engineers or executives at any facility where LANs can be installed. It eliminates the need for subjective selection, which is difficult with the bewildering number of existing systems and vendors.

2

The Evolution of Local Area Networks

The LAN concept began with the development of distributive processing in the 1970s. The first step was to interconnect two identical computers in the same building, resulting in a point-to-point network. Once the advantages of distributive processing were realized, computer networking proliferated at a rapid pace. Multipoint, star, and ring networks soon began revolutionizing the data communications field.

One of the early major developments was the U.S. Department of Defense's long distance private packet-switching network, ARPANET, in the late 1960s. ARPANET was the first major application of the then new technology called "packet switching," in which data is segmented into blocks that are separately addressed and routed independently through the network. The packet switching technology is used by some LANs today. Another major contribution of packet switching technology was the support for the concept of interconnecting dissimilar computers for data communication.

During the 70s the use of versatile and relatively inexpensive mini/microcomputers became firmly established. From office desk tops to factory floors, computing power was placed where the work was being performed. Soon the need arose for applications users to share files, programs, and storage and peripheral devices. The requirement for data exchange across departments, as well as over long distances, necessitated an increased use of data communications.

The development of a commercial LAN began at Xerox's Palo Alto Research Center in 1972 and was publicly announced as Ethernet in 1979. A cooperative effort involving Digital Equipment Corporation, Intel, and Xerox has produced an updated version of Ethernet. Since then, various other organizations have developed Ethernet "look-alikes." Ethernet began a new trend in data communications by allowing devices of different manufacturers to communicate directly with one another. The Ethernet specifications became a de facto standard for more than 30 other companies that have entered the LAN market.

CONTEMPORARY LOCAL AREA NETWORKS

LANs are one of the most promising developments in today's hi-tech communications field. LANs are discussed everywhere: at seminars, conferences, and exhibitions, and in trade magazines, newspapers, and newsletters. Exactly what constitutes a contemporary LAN is hard to define because no two persons have the same definition. Although no single definition can completely describe a LAN, the following are generalized characteristics:

- High data rates (typically 1 to 10 Mbps)
- Limited geographical scope—typically spanning about 1 kilometer
- Support of full connectivity—all devices should have the potential to communicate with each other
- Equal access by all user devices
- Ease of reconfiguration and maintenance
- Good reliability and error characteristics
- Stability under high load
- Compatibility to the greatest extent possible to a variety of equipment
- Relatively low cost

In the commercial LAN market there are over 100 companies now claiming to manufacture a product for Local Area Networking. There is a wide choice of technologies, capabilities, degrees of vendor support, and price ranges. Some of the technologies represented are traditional computer-terminal point-to-point hardwired networks that utilize the LAN concept as a marketing strategy; others are completely new technologies.

LANs received a somewhat tarnished image when some vendors announced networking capabilities before they were viable, cost effective, or even before they could be delivered. As a result, potential users became skeptical and considered LAN technology to be still in the experimental stage. With so many vendors claiming they have the panacea for networking, many potential users are exercising caution before they commit a large capital expenditure for a LAN. Some are waiting until the market matures, and to see what vendors and technologies emerge as leaders in the field. Others are waiting for the development of standards to help in their selection. Either way, organizations must still carefully choose the right LANs for their particular applications at this time.

A variety of alternative LAN designs are commercially available. Generally, one LAN is distinguished from another on the basis of (1) intended application and

Contemporary Local Area Networks 5

offered services, (2) network topology, (3) protocol architecture, and (4) transmission medium.

Application Distinctions

Almost any application implemented on a traditional point-to-point network can be converted to one of the LAN technologies. In addition, most likely new applications not generally available on a conventional network may be available to the user.

Generally, networks combine transmission, storage, and processing operations to meet specific user application requirements. The network operations requirements can roughly be divided into four areas: (1) the type of information transmitted, e.g., data and voice, (2) the type of interacting devices, e.g., terminals and computers, (3) the type of service offered, e.g., electronic mail, and (4) specialized networks, e.g., process control of laboratory automation.

Data and Voice Networks

The type of information transmitted has different characteristics. Considering voice and data, typically voice differs from data in error and buffer handling technologies as well as bandwidth requirements.

In data networks, generally two types of information transmission contribute to typical traffic patterns: (1) interactive users to and from host computers, and (2) host-to-host or to and from other intelligent devices.

In the first case, terminals operating at data rates in the 9.6K to 19.2K bps (9.6 thousand to 19.2 thousand bits-per-second) range offer bursty traffic to the network. In the second case, computers offer higher data rates. Often computer-to-computer data rates appear in bursts due to protocol overhead and the scheduling of the host processing cycles. In general, transmission of data between source and destination must be timely and error-free, usually requiring retransmission when errors are detected.

The concept of a call is appropriate to systems where a connection is made between users, held for a substantial period of time, and then broken. Implementations of voice communications have historically resulted in "circuits" where, once a connection is made, a portion of the transmission medium becomes dedicated to that circuit until a disconnect takes place. Information is transmitted without interruption in real time so that individuals on both ends continue to participate in a natural fashion; up to a point, transmission errors can be tolerated.

Voice-oriented networks historically have been designed using a variety of circuit-switching techniques. These networks make inefficient usage of circuit resources when modified to handle data.

Data-oriented networks are designed assuming computer and peripheral device interactions are transaction oriented. Individual peripheral devices typically generate a small percentage of the overall transactions. Information in these transactions is delivered in a timely manner and error-free. Data networks that carry voice must be augmented to handle these conflicting characteristics.

Integration of heterogeneous traffic into a common network is desirable for economic reasons and for simplicity of operation. Integration provides for the dynamic sharing of transmission and switching facilities and may encourage new applications such as teleconferencing.

Terminal and Computer Communications

Terminal-to-computer communications are typically transaction-oriented or "bursty," and include data entry, word processing, program development, data base access, and remote job entry. Applications require conversational network services at speeds slower than computer capabilities. Interactions are infrequent, with maximum terminal speeds of up to of 19.2 Kbps.

The primary objective of these applications is to provide geographically distributed user terminals and other types of devices with remotely located data bases and/or computing power. As a consequence, there exist two types of network nodes: those that represent terminal entry and exit points to the network and those that represent processing and data base points to the network.

Applications in which computer-to-computer communications take place are of high speed and consist of (1) file transfer and (2) distributed processing, including interprocess communications.

Computer-to-computer interactions take place at the maximum speeds allowed by the computer and network architectures, with speeds of up to 50 Mbps (50 million bits-per-second). The applications are oriented toward the same types of communication found between processes in a single computer system. These include the exchange of files and interprocess messages.

Network design and implementations are often oriented toward the highest volume of traffic required by the target installation. However, most networks require support for both types of traffic, and this implies that compromises and design trade-offs are made.

Terminal networks are generally too slow for the response required by computer-to-computer traffic. Equipment necessary to provide the high computer-to-computer speeds is more expensive than that for slower traffic types. The cost of the interface node to the network is significantly less than the device being connected.

Advanced User Services

The continuing trend of office automation is one primary reason for the proliferation of LANs.

Office automation studies underscore the need for LANs by pointing out that more than 30 percent of communication between people in an organization takes place over distances of a half mile or less. Fewer than 20 percent of communication transactions typically require long-haul transmission facilities.

The concept of office automation refers to the integration and aggregation of computer applications and office networks that aid in the performance of normal office work. Office automation includes the word processing functions (document retrieval, preparation, and editing), information storage and retrieval, electronic mail, facsimile, store-and-forward processing of digitized voice, and teleconferencing, and modeling.

Other advanced user services include general data processing–centralized file access, storage and transfer, resource sharing (e.g., peripherals, services, applications), distributed processing, distributed data base management, retail point-of-sale operations, management planning, and network management.

A word of caution: Very few vendors supply advanced user services with their networks. Often networks must be custom-developed at a large expense to the user. This requires custom software and sometimes even custom hardware. Another factor to consider is the impact of proprietary networks. Often proprietary network vendors offer advanced network services for their equipment only. Chances are that other manufacturers' equipment might not be able to connect to the network without some customizing, let alone support the advanced services. Also, what do you do when the equipment needs replacing and the vendor has gone out of business? Chances are you will need a new network. Generally, unless you are totally convinced of a manufacturer's stability, carefully investigate all facts before you purchase a proprietary LAN.

NETWORK TOPOLOGIES

The geometrical arrangement of computer resources, remote devices, and communications facilities is known as network topology. More specifically, a computer network is comprised of nodes and links. A node is the endpoint of any branch in a computer network and can take the form of a computer, a terminal device, a work station, a miscellaneous device, or an interconnecting equipment facility. A link is a communication path between two nodes. (The terms "circuit" and "channel" are frequently used as synonyms for link.) When a computer network is designed, its topology is determined by the following considerations: functional objectives, reliability requirements, and operational costs.

Unlike long-haul networks, which usually support an unconstrained topology, most LANs have a specific topology with which they are designed to operate. With standard networks there are two basic network types: the point-to-point connection and the multipoint connection. In a point-to-point connection two nodes are connected through a single communications link, so that one communications channel exists for that link. In a multipoint connection, several nodes share the same communications link, but only one node can transmit at a time. Most LANs, on the other hand, utilize a "broadcast" topology in which multi-addressing is employed, but they can also utilize the point-to-point and multipoint concept. All messages are physically transmitted to every network station, but each station only acts upon those messages addressed to itself. This contrasts with the point-to-point and multipoint concept in which a central node services each station one at a time, and each message is transmitted only to its addressee. The most common LAN topologies are the ring,

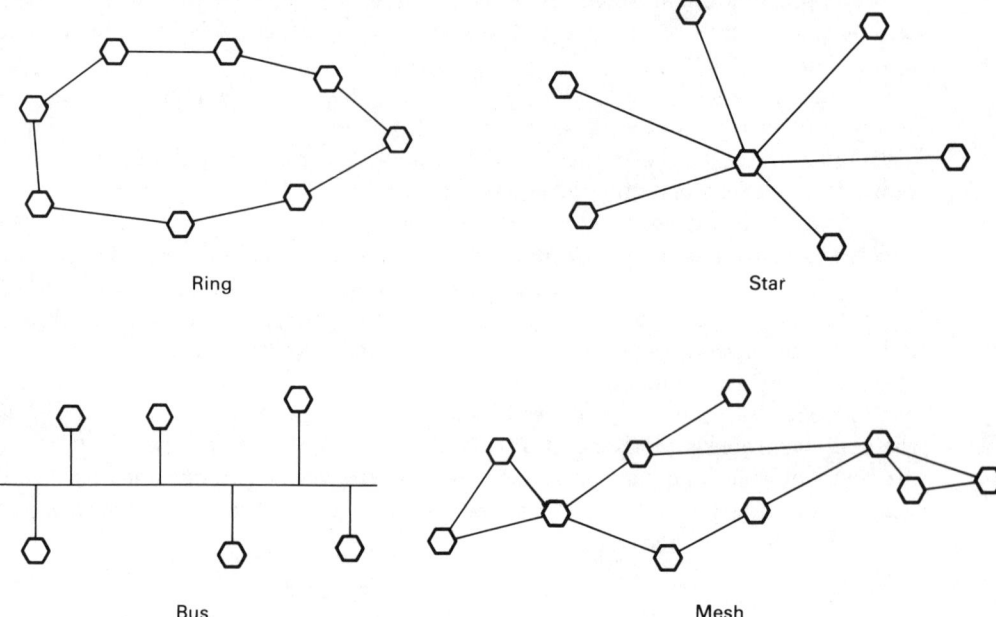

Figure 2-1 Network Topologies

the star, the bus, and the mesh, which are discussed as follows and are represented in Figure 2-1.

Ring Topologies

The distinguishing feature of ring topologies is that the nodes, which are connected by point-to-point links, are arranged to form a closed, circular configuration. With a full duplex link, nodes are able to transmit and receive data in either direction on the ring, but data must pass through all nodes between the sender and the receiver with the possibility of a shorter path in one direction or the other. Unidirectional ring topologies are more common. When messages are sent from one node to any other, they are transmitted onto the ring and travel around it until received at the addressed node or returned to the transmitting node. Each node must be able to recognize its own address in order to accept messages. In addition, each node serves as an active repeater, retransmitting messages addressed to other nodes.

Unidirectional ring topologies have the following characteristics:

- Message routing is simplified, since only one message path is possible, considering the most common implementation.
- A transmitting node need only know an identifier for the receiving node, and not its location.

- Broadcast message transmission is easy to achieve, since every node is capable of receiving the message as long as previous nodes have not removed it from the ring.
- Capital investment can be low, with cost proportional to the number of users or interfaces.
- The possibility for high throughput exists, since more than one message can be in transit at once.

Ring topologies are categorized according to the type of message transmission mechanism employed. Examples of transmission mechanisms are

1. The round-robin passing of a control token from one node to the next, where only the node with the token can transmit an arbitrary length message.
2. The slotted ring in which fixed-sized slots are cycled around the ring; with a bit indicating whether the slot is full or empty, the node can fill a slot as required (demand multiplexing) or can be assigned a specific slot or set of slots (synchronous time division multiplexing).

In any ring control strategy there is some entity, be it a control token or an explicit signal on a wire, that is passed from node to node to indicate which node currently has the right to transmit. The strategy takes into consideration the possibility that a transient error may destroy the entity, and therefore the entity must be prepared to restart itself after such an error. This is accomplished by regenerating the permission to send and bestowing it uniquely upon one of the nodes. While it is difficult to determine with certainty that the control entity has been lost and to decide which node should take it upon itself to recreate it, solutions do exist; usually, these solutions include some form of contention.

Transmission and processing errors can affect proper network operation as in the following example. If a message is somehow distorted with the address modified, the message could be delivered to the wrong destination. An invalid address, if not properly handled by the system, may result in a message that continues to circulate around the ring. Many systems use varying monitoring schemes to check and remove these messages.

Performance of a ring network is dependent upon the message transmission mechanism. A simplistic mechanism may require each node to take messages into buffers as they are passed from node to node in order to interrogate an address field. If heavy traffic conditions exist, messages may have to wait in long queues at each node for input and/or output. Delay is a fixed function dependent on the number of nodes and the node processing time. Single or multiple node failure could either cause a loss of access to the ring or a breakdown in total operation. Potentially low reliability can be compensated by high quality engineering design.

Expansion is usually simple. It requires the insertion (electrical) of the new node's interface into the ring. It also involves identifying the new address to the neighboring nodes.

Rings provide the best performance for networks with a small number of nodes operating at high speeds over short distances. The token ring in general performs well, as long as implementations result in low delay at each station. Backbone rates of 100 Mbps and more are possible.

Star Topologies

The only nonbroadcast topology currently available in the commercial LAN market is the star. The star topology consists of a central node to which every other node is linked via point-to-point connection. The central node controls and routes all network traffic (e.g., when messages are sent between the network nodes, the transmitting node makes the request to the central node, which in turn establishes a path to the receiving node). Star topology networks are of two types, circuit switched or message switched.

With circuit switching, the link between the transmitting and receiving nodes is established on demand for exclusive use of the circuit until the connection is released. The modern PBX systems that handle voice and data are circuit switched networks.

With message switching, the entire message is transmitted to an intermediate point (i.e., switching computer), stored for a period of time (usually short), and then transmitted again toward its destination. The destination of each message is indicated by an address field in the message. Store-and-forward processing is typical of contemporary distributed processing systems made up of a number of stars, where the central computer of one star has the capability to communicate with central computers of other stars often located some distance away.

Single-node failures present minimal reliability problems, since the remaining portion of the network is still able to function. Failure of the central switch, unless implemented with full redundancy, brings the entire network to a halt.

A single star configuration may be expanded up to the limitations of the central switch. Configurations grow in terms of switching capacity (number of switches that can be made in a given amount of time), numbers of concurrent circuits that may be maintained, and total number of nodes that may be serviced. Switching capacity depends upon the message rate, throughput, and the processing time required for each message.

Throughput in a star topology network is the time required for the central switch to process and route a message. Message processing time depends upon the number of network nodes and message length. The throughput rate is the reciprocal of the sum of processing time and input and output buffering times. Using software-implemented switches, current PBX systems typically handle 2000–4000 concurrent circuits, with devices communicating at effective speeds of up to 56 Kbps.

Bus Topologies

The bus topology is currently more popular than the ring topology, largely due to the influences of Xerox's Ethernet and the wide acceptance of coaxial cable-oriented transmission medium. With the bus, network nodes connect to a linear length of cable

Control and Access

to which user stations are connected by network interface units. Each network interface unit has a unique identifier address for receipt of transmitted messages.

There are a variety of ways to arbitrate the use of the bus. They can be classified as either centralized or distributed centralized control schemes, utilizing a master node or a dedicated bus controller. Centrally controlled bus topologies are not common for LANs. In decentralized bus topology, the control logic is distributed throughout all the nodes connected to the bus. It is the most commonly used method.

Because of the passive role the nodes play in transmissions on the bus, generally a node can fail without affecting the operations of the entire network. This makes distributed networks almost inherently resistant to single point failure.

The reliability of a bus network depends on the topology and the control strategy. When using various types of contention control, almost all failures have the same effect as a collison, which is usually handled automatically depending on network configuration and management. Network performance is determined by bus bandwidth, number of nodes, access protocols and the type, average, and peak user data traffic.

Bus structure expandability primarily depends on the transmission medium, and expansion may require the addition of amplifiers or repeaters accordingly. Hardware and software characteristics must be considered, but generally bus structures are easily reconfigured and expanded.

A variation of the bus is the tree topology which splits the bus into different segments. Bridging devices are used to connect the segments. Reliability and performance characteristics are similar to the bus.

Mesh Topologies

Mesh topologies, also called unconstrained or hybrid, are nonspecific network configurations. The actual connections make up the geometric shape and can vary from one implementation to another, the resulting configuration usually being the most economical one. Mesh topologies can be made up of point-to-point and multipoint data links creating redundant data paths. Nodes can be routing or nonrouting depending on the topology.

Performance characteristics of a mesh network utilizing adaptive routing techniques are difficult to predict and often involve complex simulation models. Expandability is relatively easy as long as the connecting nodes can handle the additional traffic. Mesh topologies are not widely used for LANs; they are more commonly used for long-haul packet networks.

Figure 2-2 summarizes the characteristics of the ring, star, bus, and mesh topologies.

CONTROL AND ACCESS

Control and access techniques, along with the network topologies, are utilized to obtain the desired performance and operational requirements for the network applica-

Topology	User interface complexity	Expandability	Flexibility	Reliability
Bus	Low to moderate	High	High	High
Ring	Low	Moderate	Moderate	High
Star	Low	Low	Low	Moderate to high
Tree	Moderate	High	High	High
Mesh	High	Very high	Very high	Moderate

Figure 2-2 Topology Characteristics Summary

tions. Control of the network is either centralized in a single master node or distributed to all the nodes. Access techniques are the way in which the nodes obtain the use of a common channel to transmit data. The two common methods are contention oriented or noncontention oriented. Specifically, they can be classified as statistical and deterministic.

Polling

Polling techniques are a noncontention form of channel access. In a deterministic way each node can gain access to the channel, and direct conflict between the nodes is avoided. The form of polling most often used is centralized polling in which the master node queries each node in turn. If the node has a message to transmit, it sends the message; if not, the master polls the next node, and so on. The order in which the nodes are polled can be arbitrary, based on physical location, or a priority system can be used.

Polling techniques using centrally controlled polling can be implemented in any topology. Another common form of polling is distributed polling in which each node can control its access to the network. The most common form used in LANs is token passing, which is described in the following discussion.

Token Passing

Token passing can be considered as a form of distributed polling. It is often implemented in ring topologies, but is gaining acceptance with bus networks as well. The token ring technique utilizes a special bit pattern, known as a token, which is passed from one node to the next sequentially around the network. A node with a message to transmit has a specific amount of time to remove the token, accept a message, or add a message to it. During this time, all other network nodes can only listen to the network. This process continues until the original sending node receives the token from the last network node and acknowledges that the intended recipient received

Transmission Mediums 13

the message. Token passing guarantees access to the network in a predetermined amount of time, making it more suitable for command control, process, or other real-time applications than contention methods.

Contention Techniques

Contention techniques allow nodes to gain access to the channel in a statistical manner. One of the more publicized methods is carrier sense multiple access with collison detection (CSMA/CD). CSMA/CD requires the nodes to listen before transmitting. If another station is transmitting, the listening node or station will either back off for a specified time interval before listening again, or will continuously monitor until the network is clear to send. If a collision occurs during transmission because two stations began sending simultaneously, both sending nodes will back off for random time intervals before trying again. The waiting time distribution is influenced by such factors as network traffic volume, message length, and network physical length. This method has the advantage of treating all stations in the network as having equal priority.

TRANSMISSION MEDIUMS

The transmission medium is the physical connection which interconnects the network nodes, allowing the user devices to send and receive messages. Generally transmission media can be classified into two categories: bounded and unbounded. Bounded media include twisted pair, baseband and broadband coaxial cable, and fiber optic cable. Unbounded media include radio waves, microwaves, and infrared transmissions. In general, most LANs used bounded media.

Twisted Pair

Multiwire twisted pair is the simplest transmission technique. It is also the most familiar, because it is the transmission medium used in commercial PBX telephone systems. The most common type used is two-pair wire, which consists of two pairs of plastic-sheathed copper wire twisted around one another, then wrapped with a protective outer sheath. Twisted wire is the least expensive medium. Twisted pair wire can be used with any of the basic topologies, and typical networks contain up to 255 user devices. Either an analog or a digital signal can be transmitted, depending on the type of modulation used.

Bandwidth varies depending on the distance between repeaters, signaling technique, and quality of the wire. Data rates up to 1.5 Mbps can be achieved; however, today's typical PBX systems operate at 56K or 64 Kbps, with end user devices communicating at 9600 bps over point-to-point connections, or 1200 bps over multipoint connections. At lower data rates, the bit error rate is also low, but as the data rate increases, so does the error rate. Signals for several devices can be multiplexed onto a single wire using time division or frequency division multiplexing techniques.

The main advantage of a hardwire system is lower costs; however, the system is not as flexible as either baseband or broadband, due to frequency limitations.

Baseband Coaxial Cable

Baseband coaxial cable transmits a single digital signal in half-duplex mode only. No frequency modulation takes place as in broadband transmission, but the raw bit stream is usually specially modified before transmission, using techniques such as Manchester encoding. The absolute maximum data rate supported is 50 Mbps, since it may occupy the full available cable bandwidth of 50 MHz; however, typical practical maximums range from 3 Mbps to 10 Mbps.

Baseband cable is generally used only with linear bus topologies. A typical network contains 200 to 1000 devices. A baseband network has an upper length of 1000 to 4000 feet. In order to extend the network to connect to other buildings in a campus style, it is necessary to use one or more other baseband networks with "gateways" (involving repeaters) to connect them.

Multiple messages can travel on the cable simultaneously using time division multiplexing techniques. Although baseband LANs are designed primarily for data communications, limited non-real-time voice and video applications, such as voice store-and-forward and freeze-frame video, can be accommodated by digitizing the voice or data signal. Baseband cable is considered a "passive" medium in that all electrical power used to drive the network is provided by the user stations.

In summary, a baseband network is a dedicated network designed for one type of use. The basic use is for short, bursty communications between computers, terminals, and peripherals, where speed of access does not have to be guaranteed. No other signals, such as analog voice signals, can share the same network. Lengthy operations, such as file transfers, delay other users' access to the network; simultaneous transmissions are not possible.

Broadband Coaxial Cable

A broadband local network is basically a radio-frequency-based multiple-channel medium, capable of accommodating the two general types of communications traffic: (1) bursty, delay-critical communications, such as interactive communications between a terminal and a computer, and (2) lengthy communications such as voice, file transfers, and teleconferencing.

Broadband coaxial cable and its related components used in local data networks are the same as those used in commercial residential cable television networks. The cable, which has an available bandwidth of almost 400 MHz, transmits a signal that contains multiple independent channels defined by frequency division multiplexing techniques. The LAN may use the standard 6 MHz community antenna television (CATV) channels defined for commercial cable TV, or specially allocated vendor-defined channels that are not consistent with commercial CATV standards. Each channel can be designated for voice, video, or data transmission, and the cable can carry all three types of channels simultaneously, resulting in a multifunction signal. Unlike baseband, both real-time voice and video applications are supported.

The cable signal is in radio-frequency (RF) analog mode, and therefore data must be modulated before transmission, using an RF modem. All signals are half-duplex, but full transmission can be achieved by using two channels. Because of amplification and channel splitting, broadband cable has a much higher workstation capacity and greater geographic scope than baseband networks. Some broadband networks can support up to 25,000 workstations, and maximum distance can be in the 50-mile range.

Broadband cable is considered an "active" medium, in that the electrical power used to drive the network is based in the network components, rather than in the user stations as in baseband networks. Most broadband LANs support industry-standard CATV equipment for the internal components of the network. Installation of a broadband cable and related components is more difficult than installation of a baseband network.

All broadband networks function in a similar manner: transmitted carrier signals are sent to a central point (headend) from which they are transmitted to all points on the network. To accomplish this bidirectionality, two different cable schemes are used: single-cable and dual-cable, which we will now discuss.

Single-cable schemes employ only one cable, which uses a frequency-spectrum split to achieve bidirectional communications. The available frequency range is split into a return band from the user to the headend and a forward band from the headend to the user.

Single-cable networks can be represented as a branching tree, which simplifies network design and also facilitates network maintenance. A technician can easily trace such a topology.

A dual-cable network is represented by a single cable that makes a physical loop at the headband, thus creating two separate cable paths: inbound and outbound.

The normal dual-cable–frequency-spectrum coverage is from 54 to 400 MHz, for a total of 346 MHz. This provides twice the bandwidth of a single cable system. Not all dual-cable networks conform to the same bandpass. For example, Wang Laboratories' Wangnet uses a frequency-spectrum coverage of 10 to 350 MHz for a total bandwidth of 340 MHz.

Dual-cable installations provide more difficult network design and maintenance problems. Noise accumulation increases with cable length and the number of line amplifiers. Essentially, the cable has double the length and number of amplifiers of a single-cable system, providing considerably more noise. Designing to reduce the number of amplifiers and cable length becomes more important.

Maintenance requirements for both single- and dual-cable networks are very low due to the high reliability and mean time between failures of the RF components. However, once the dual-cable loop is branched, the physical tracing of the loop and differentiating of cables becomes even more difficult.

Dual-cable networks normally are not as cost-effective as single-cable networks, mainly because they require twice the cabling, hardware, and amplifier chassis to support the same number of outlets. It may also be difficult to find the required space to mount or service all the dual-cable network components.

Fiber Optic Cable

Fiber optic cable has a central core of glass or plastic with a high index of refraction. This fiber is surrounded by a cladding layer of a slightly lower refractive index, which isolates the central fiber from other fibers. Each fiber provides a single, unidirectional, end-to-end transmission path. Lasers and light-emitting diodes are used for the light-wave transmission. The transmission is usually point-to-point in digital baseband. Practical data rates of up to 50 Mbps have been realized over a distance of six miles without repeaters.

There are many advantages to fiber optic transmission. It is unaffected by electrical interference, noise, crosstalk, power outages, and short circuits, and tolerant of adverse temperatures, chemicals, and radiation. Even in the current state of the technology, bandwidth is much higher than with any other medium. Any type of signal can be encoded—voice, data, or video. The cable is highly secure, since it is difficult to tap. Physically, the cable is small in diameter, light in weight, durable, and able to fit into limited duct space.

Although there are many advantages, a few disadvantages make current implementation impractical for most commercial LANs. The cable is still quite expensive—in the range upwards of seven dollars per foot. Installing and maintaining are not easy and require highly skilled personnel. However, the most significant disadvantage is that the taps are not perfected, and high signal loss and low reliability often result. The problems are expected to be worked out in the next few years, resulting in the probability of fiber optics as the future LAN transmission medium.

Figure 2-3 summarizes and compares LAN transmission mediums.

NETWORK ARCHITECTURE AND COMMUNICATION STANDARDS

In a LAN, it is highly desirable that machines of different manufacturers be able to communicate. For this to be possible, they must conform to certain standards. The National Bureau of Standards (NBS) is currently developing a set of LAN standards which will be based on the International Standards Organization (ISO) reference model. The Institute of Electrical and Electronic Engineers (IEEE) 802 Technical Committee is also developing a set of standards which will include standards for media access as well as media standards for twisted pair wiring plus baseband and broadband coaxial cable.

The ISO Reference Model

Figure 2-4, ISO Seven-Layer Architectural Model, illustrates the types of layers which are fundamental to advanced teleprocessing systems. Layer 1 is the physical (electrical) connection between the data machines and the network. Layer 2 is the link con-

Network Architecture and Communications Standards

Media	Bandwidth	Distance	Topological versatility	Ease of installation	Noise immunity
Twisted pair	Low	Low	High	Moderate	Low
Baseband coax	Low to moderate	Moderate	High	High	Moderate
Broadband coax	High	High	High	High	High
Fiber optic	High	Very high	Moderate	Moderate	Very high

Figure 2-3 Transmission Media Summary and Comparison

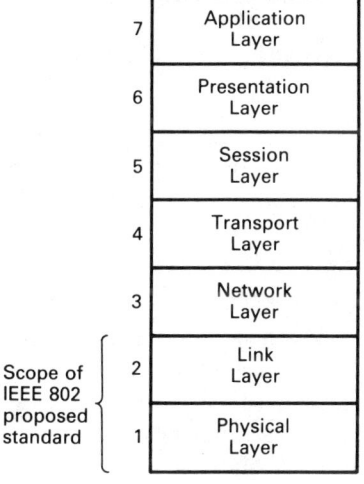

Figure 2-4 ISO Seven-Layer Architectural Model

trol which relates to the way data is transmitted over the LAN. Layers 3 and 4, in conjunction with the three lower layers, provide the transmission subsystem. These first four layers can be regarded as the entity which the upper levels use to move data from one machine to another. The following is a brief description of the various layers in the model:

Layer 1: Physical. This layer provides the physical, electrical, functional, and procedural characteristics to establish, maintain, and disconnect the physical link. Examples of the physical connections would be the interface between a terminal and a network interface unit (NIU) and the interface between the NIU and the network. Examples of the electrical interfaces would be voltage levels or pulse lengths. Some of the standards of Layer 1 are: RS-232, RS-422, RS-423, RS-449, V.24, and X.21.

Layer 2: Link Control. This layer concerns sending blocks of data over a physical link. The link control procedure specifies the headers and trailers of data blocks and defines a protocol for the movement of these blocks. Specific examples of functions within these layers include: error detection and correction, message addressing, and block framing. Some of the standards are Higher-level Data Link Control (HDLC) for bit-oriented messages and ANSI X3.28 for character-oriented messages.

Layer 3: Network. This layer provides virtual circuits for the exchange of data and control between users and the network. As an example, the user may transmit data in packets that are transmitted over several different physical links and are then reassembled in order for reception by another user. Layer 3 provides a virtual circuit between the user and the network. The standard associated with this layer is X.25.

Layer 4: Transport. This layer is concerned with the end-to-end interaction between user processes. The functions provided may include end-to-end integrity controls to prevent loss or double processing of transactions, flow control of transactions, and sequence control.

This layer and those below it transport the blocks of bits from one user to another.

Layer 5: Session. This layer establishes, maintains, and terminates a dialog session between two users. A protocol regulates which user transmits and for how long, how interrupts are handled, and in what order transmission occurs.

Layer 6: Presentation. This layer provides for the transformation of information being processed to a form acceptable for the application layer. This function transforms data bits to a readable display or print-out. Other functions in this layer could include data encryption and decryption, data compaction and expansion, and code conversion.

Layer 7: Application. This layer is concerned with higher-level functions which support system activities such as file transfer control, distributed data-base activities, and operator support. Some of the controls at this layer are time-sharing of transactions and delivery of transactions in time-share sequence. Examples include remote job entry and electronic mail.

Although the IEEE 802 proposed standard is compatible with only the first two layers of the seven-layer ISO OSI (Open Systems Interconnection) reference model, work is proceeding to have LANs eventually compatible with all seven layers. The ISO OSI reference model represents the ideal case, something few computer and peripheral manufacturers can be expected to support completely. Most manufacturers have generally adopted the first two layers; very few provide Level 3 and above services.

In summary, network requirements in the standards area are linked to the developing IEEE and NBS standards. The LAN architecture should be designed so that as these standards are adopted, they can be implemented with minimum impact.

3

Model Approach to Local Area Network Design

A typical computer network is defined as a collection of resources, each of which can perform work at some finite rate, connected to a collection of users who demand work from these resources in some random fashion. The network is a collection of nodes at which reside the resources which are connected into the network through network interface units (NIUs). Messages in the form of commands, inquiries, and file transmissions travel over the channels. The NIUs perform the tasks of relaying messages (with appropriate routing, acknowledging, error and flow controlling, queuing, etc.) and of inserting and removing messages that originate and terminate at the terminals and main processors.

The total network may be partitioned into sub-networks: (1) the LAN providing the message service and (2) the collection of user devices that form the user-resource network (URN). A LAN is made up of (a) a physical network consisting of the transmission lines and amplifiers; (b) a message network (defined by origin, destination, origination time, length, priority class, etc.) that moves messages through the physical network in a store-and-forward fashion; and (c) the control network for monitoring and controlling the flow of this message traffic.

In order to represent a resource-sharing LAN as a model, the network topology can best be viewed as an arbitrary number of interconnected nodes, each node consisting of one or more user devices connected to an independent NIU. In the model portrayed in this chapter, the user devices will be defined as all sources and destinations of all network messages, and will represent central processing units (CPUs), terminals, printers, concentrators, modems, and gateways to other networks. The NIU's role is to handle all conceivable communication functions, such as message switching, error correction, and buffering. Figure 3-1, Total Network, illustrates the component breakdown of a typical network.

1. **Local Area Network**

    Baseband and Broadband   *Digital PBX*

    (a) Physical Network
           Transmission Lines   Transmission Lines
           Amplifiers   Amplifiers
           Equalizers   Multiplexers
           Power Supplies   Power Supplies
           Splitters
           Directional Couplers
           Taps
           Drops

    (b) Message Network
           Network Interface Units (NIUs)   Main Switch Unit
           RF Modems
           Translators (up/down converters)
             or Directors
           Bridges (channel to channel)

    (c) Control Network
           Monitors (status, line, throughout)   Master Control Unit
           Configuration Controllers
             (assignment)

2. **User Resource Network (User Devices)**
       Terminals
       Gateways
       Computers
       Modems
       Printers
       Video Terminals

Figure 3–1 Total Network

TECHNICAL APPROACH

The technical approach used in determining the physical network is the same for any design. After establishing the type of LAN and the physical aspects, the model is used to provide information for sizing the message network. The various parameters developed in determining the physical network are used where applicable in this design. The control network is then designed to support the operational use of the LAN and the model. The model may then be used for dynamic reconfiguration.

Physical Network Technical Approach

Figure 3–2 represents the technical approach used in the alternative designs of the physical network as presented in the following chapters.

    The LAN requirements are determined by analyzing the existing, planned, and

Technical Approach

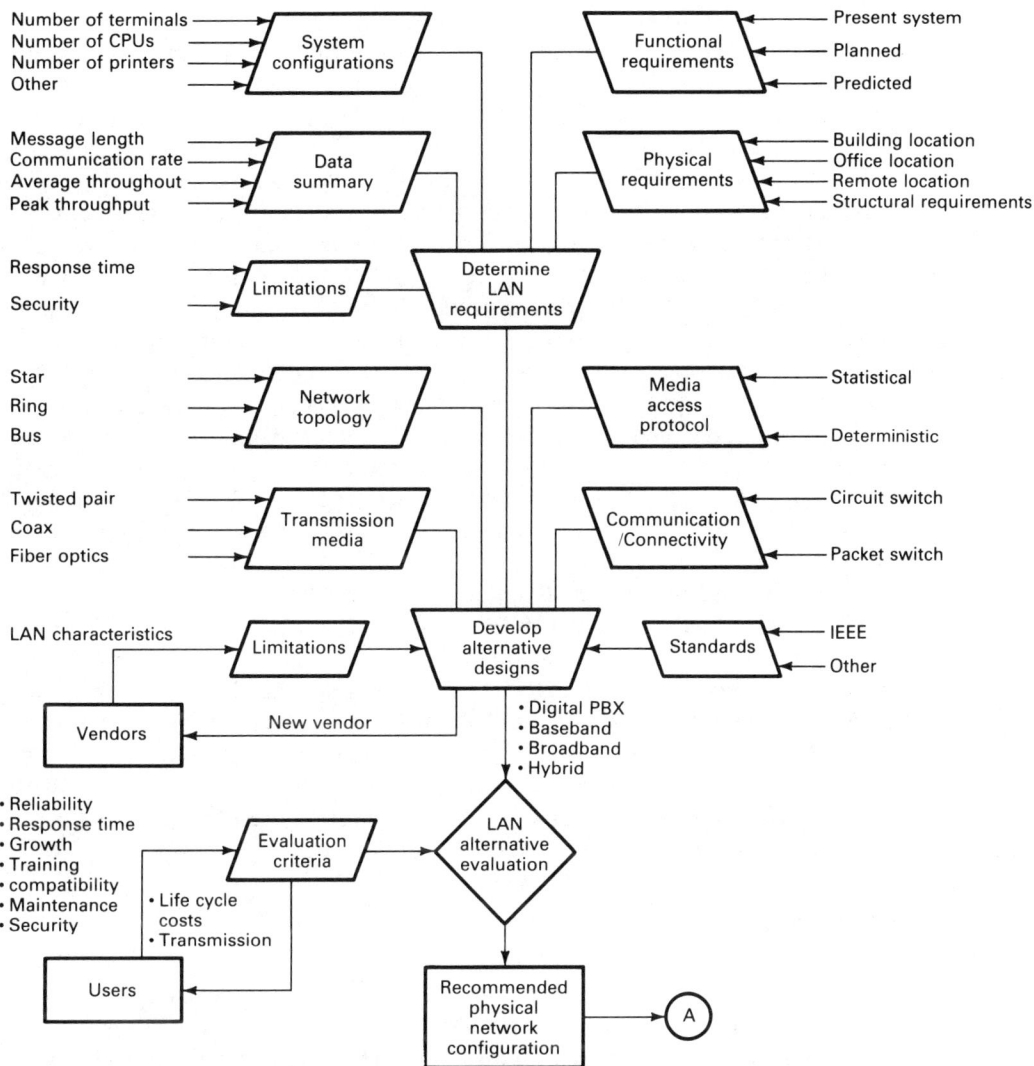

Figure 3-2 LAN Model, Physical Network Model Technical Approach

predicted systems, as well as physical environment for these systems. Next, the hardware configuration of each system is analyzed. Estimates are made of the number of terminals, CPUs, and other devices. The functional requirements are then defined and the input and output data for each system calculated in terms of message length, communication rate, average throughput, and peak throughout. Limitations in regard to response time and security are used to modify the previous data where necessary. The summation of all these data then constitutes the requirements for the LAN.

The next step in this technical approach is to develop several alternatives designs of a LAN that would satisfy the previously determined requirements. A number of transmission media used by LAN vendors, such as twisted pair wire, coaxial cable, and fiber optics, are to be studied and evaluated. Network topology and its relationships to the transmission media must be analyzed. Similarly, the media access protocol must be analyzed in relation to the various network media and topologies. The choices of protocol are limited to those supported by the more viable vendors. All vendors supporting a statistical approach to acquiring access to the LAN media use the Carrier Sense Multiple Access (CSMA) or CSMA with Collision Detection (CSMA/CD) approach. Most of the vendors supporting a deterministic approach use token passing for their protocol, although there are a number of variations in this method of polling. Communication connectivity should also be analyzed; however, the means of establishing the communication path, i.e., packet switching or circuit switching, is dependent upon the transmission media, network topology, and LAN vendor equipment.

As yet, standards have not been established for LANs; therefore, assumptions must be made in the development of alternative designs that will satisfy the requirements for the LAN. These designs are categorized as digital PBX, baseband, broadband, and a hybrid of the broadband and baseband networks.

The following method for evaluating these four designs has been developed and can be applied to any network system design. Evaluation criteria are selected and, through a reiteration process with the user, a fixed weight can be established for each criterion. Each alternative design can be rated independently using these weighted criteria and, after a comparison is made, a specific design is chosen on the basis of the weighted ratings. This selection represents the LAN physical network and, together with the parameters leading to this configuration, becomes the basis for the conceptual design of the message and control networks.

Message Network Technical Approach

The technical approach used in designing a message network includes a mathematical model for determining the mean throughput rate and message delay as functions of the number of user devices. This information is then used to determine the number of channels and the number of user devices per channel based upon optimum throughput and delay. The message network can then be designed from this information, as the type and number of translators and bridges are dependent upon the number of channels. Figure 3-3 represents this technical approach.

Input to the mathematical model includes requirements and network design data as previously defined, plus transmittal characteristics and algorithm assumptions. Some of the transmittal characteristics include packet size and format, channel noise, packet arrival process, and retransmission process. Some of the algorithm assumptions include mathematical formulas for maximum mean throughput, mean delay, and mean transfer rate. The user devices represent any origin or destination of messages. They generate and consume messages in a process defined by input to the model.

Technical Approach

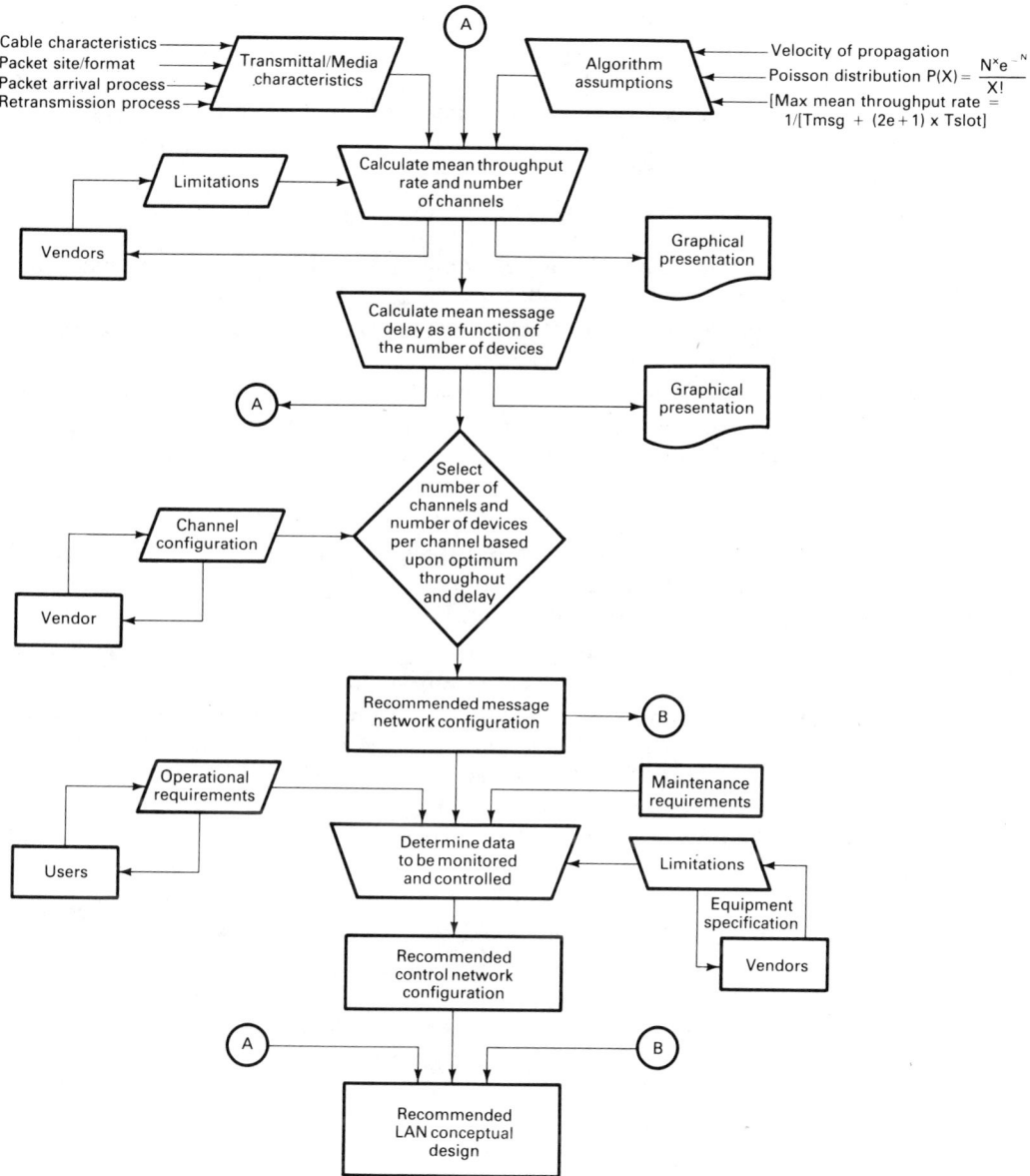

Figure 3-3 LAN Model, Message and Control Network Model Technical Approach

Peak data rates are used in all calculations. The message size is of random length as defined by input; however, maximum length is determined by hardware limits. The output of the mathematical model is in the form of graphical presentations to be used for selecting the optimum number of user devices per channel. A trade-off exists where increased channels to optimize the number of user devices require additional translators and bridges, thereby increasing costs and delay time. This analysis is done empirically. In a full operational status, the analysis of the network is performed dynamically, using information derived from the control network.

Control Network Technical Approach

Network management is an important function of a LAN once it is operational. This is the portion of the LAN that provides the managerial interface with the URN. Network management gathers usage information for planning and control purposes and provides status information for maintenance of both the LAN and the URN. A LAN can function without a control network if considerable preplanning is accomplished in the development of the physical and message network, the workload does not change, and there are relatively few maintenance problems. However, complete preplanning is not always possible due to the dynamic changes in the URN. Workloads often change for the same reason.

The technical approach used in designing a control network is empirical in nature. There is no mathematical methodology for determining types or amount of monitoring and control equipment. Input consists of data requirements to support operational and maintenance groups. An operations group requires data on channel and subchannel utilization, error rates, retransmission ratios, and packet sizes, plus specific user device information to control use of the user resource. A maintenance group requires data on physical and message network equipment status. Selection of data to be monitored and information to be developed will be dependent upon the network management equipment available from vendors.

The control network design can be upgraded at any time after the physical and message networks are installed. The control network can be added to or modified without altering the other networks, thereby always insuring that the latest hardware and software technology is present on the network.

Determining Local Area Network Requirements

The primary purpose of a LAN is to provide a fully integrated, flexible communications network capable of meeting an organization's evolving data communications needs. Ideally, the LAN can serve as a common interface between equipment of different types and/or manufacturers, thus freeing the user from dependence on a single-vendor environment.

REQUIRED SERVICES

Potentially, the network will support full connectivity, with every user level of the network being able to communicate with every other device. Although full connectivity would be the ideal goal, the network itself will not solve all the problems of interoperability. Complete interoperability requires application compatibility not provided by the network. The network simply provides the electrical connectivity, and perhaps some low-level protocols. To the user, the network will be application-transparent and appear as a communications pipeline.

Functional Requirements

The LAN usually consists of related and nonrelated system applications, all sharing the same transmission medium. Although the LAN will be applications-transparent between the different functional systems, the network should be able to support the following applications to all users:

- Electronic mail and calendar management
- Word processing

- Management information system
- Facsimile
- Data entry
- Voice mail

In addition to supporting the above-mentioned applications, the LAN should have the following features as a minimum:

- Menu driven network
- Security
- Modular design for expansion
- Gateways to other networks (networks and individual systems as required)
- Network growth capacity

Physical Requirements

The LAN may encompass several buildings. Figures 4-1 and 4-2 illustrate a typical physical layout that will be used as an example throughout this text. Measurements are critical, as will be illustrated in later chapters. Another chart, Figure 4-3, shows the number of offices per building per floor in the typical layout. These layouts are merely basic building blocks in the design of a LAN. The examples shown throughout this text are from an actual study conducted by the authors.

Supported Equipment

The typical LAN is often required to support various types of equipment, based on the individual system applications. Types of equipment requiring support minimally include

- Terminals
- Computers
- Peripherals: printers, storage units, tape drives, and special equipment
- Gateways to systems external to the LAN

Terminal support is required for applications desiring terminal-to-terminal communications. Such support can be either through network interface units, allowing terminals to attach to the network directly, or through a host CPU. This allows terminals of varying characteristics to communicate with the host applications.

Support of particular computers is a more difficult issue, since certain computers may require a specialized interface. Although custom interfaces are to be avoided if possible, special applications may require them.

Required Services

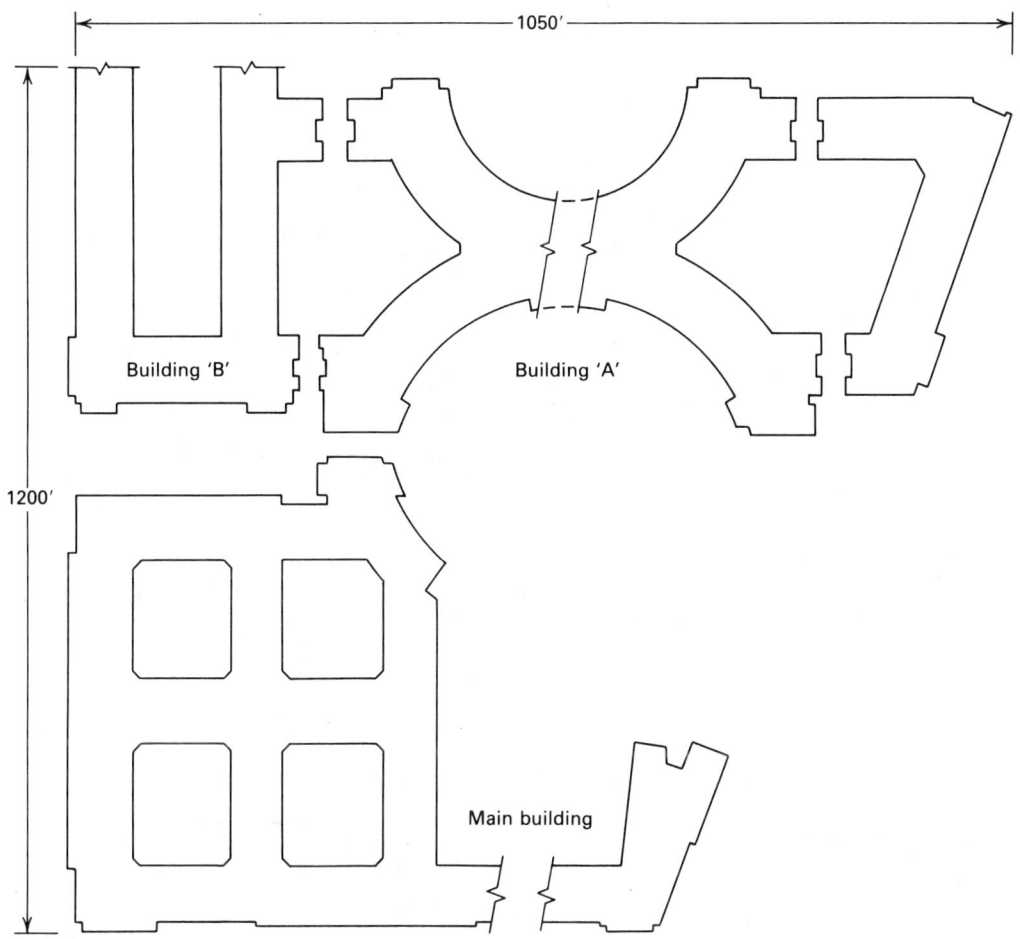

Figure 4-1 Facility Layout

Interface Requirements

If the proposed systems requiring network support are in the feasibility or planning stages, specific types of equipment cannot be identified. Therefore, the major constraining factors limiting the types of equipment supported by the network are the network interface requirements as defined by the vendors.

Digital Devices. Data communications standards may be placed in three categories: interfaces, protocols, and higher-level network controls.

Interface standards at the physical level are well established and represent one of the more stable areas of standardization. These standards define the electrical characteristics, e.g., voltage levels and grounding arrangements, and mechanical specifications, e.g., pin connector design, cable lengths, and other functions associated with physically connecting data communications equipment.

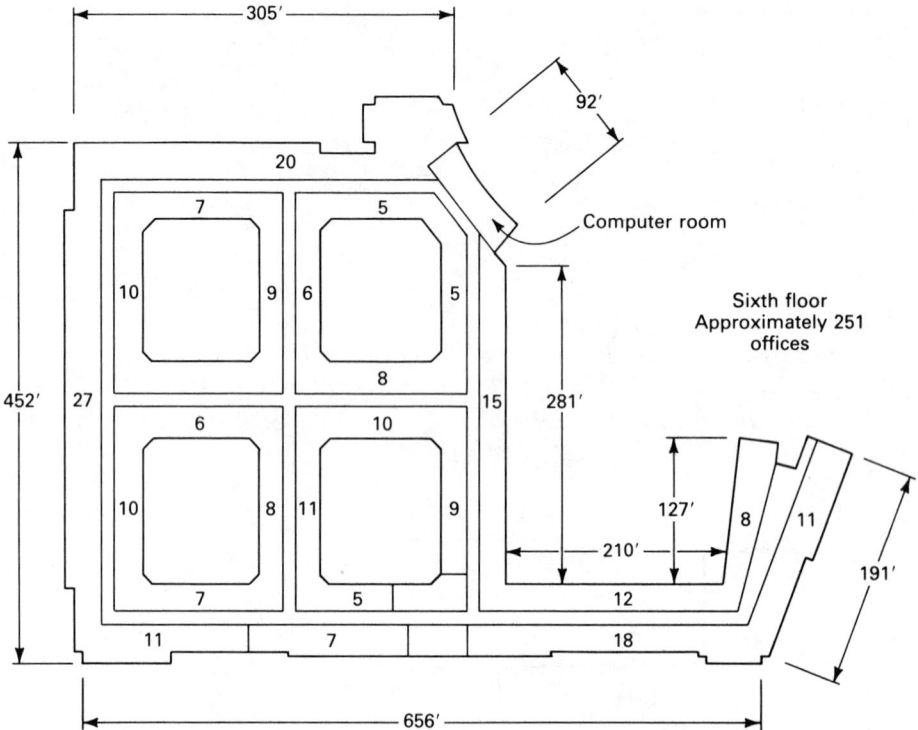

Figure 4-2 Typical Office Location Layout, Main Building

Floor	Main Building	Building 'A'	Building 'B'
7	128	102	N/A
6	256	110	75
5	256	85	N/A
4	256	N/A	N/A
3	256	N/A	N/A
2	256	54	N/A
1	256	7	N/A
B	128	N/A	N/A
Total	1792	358	75

Figure 4-3 Estimated Number of Offices Per Building

At the physical level, the data terminal equipment will be required to conform to the generic standards such as EIA* RS-232-C and 449, or to the compatible international standards, CCITT+ X.24, X.21, and ISO 2110. The LAN should support various classes of terminals and workstations (e.g., asynchronous, synchronous) which will vary widely in capabilities and data transfer requirements.

There are two basic alternatives for a LAN interface to the host computers.

---

*Electronic Industries Association
+Consultative Committee for International Telephone and Telegraph

Required Services 29

One alternative utilizing a low data rate (19.2 Kbps or less) is for the NIU to appear as a terminal to the host. Changes to the host software would be minimal but functionally the interface would be limited to terminal access, and the line speeds available would inhibit communications between LAN hosts.

Another alternative where host-to-host data transfers are involved is a high data rate NIU. The LAN interface unit would appear as an intelligent peripheral (such as a front-end processor) to the host. A high data rate NIU would support many logical connections over a serial or parallel interface. This approach has the advantage of being able to support process-to-process applications, such as file-transfer-resource-sharing between two LAN hosts. The major difficulty in this approach is the host-specific hardware and software required.

The host interface requirements should be standardized as much as possible to prevent the need for customized interfaces. At the hardware level, the host interface requirements should follow the specifications for a high-speed parallel interface, such as the IEEE 488 or the FIPS 60 I/O channel interface.

In the design of your system, develop a summary of the digital devices pertinent to the LAN. An example is presented in Figure 4-4. This summary reflects the number of CPUs, terminals, and printers relative to each of the systems which will be integrated with the LAN.

Non-Digital Devices. The LAN may also be required to support nondigital devices for multimachine applications. The integration of nondigital (e.g., video, voice, and facsimile) with digital devices is not a common occurrence. However, it is anticipated that more and more in the future the requirements will include nondigital devices. The following are assumptions affecting how voice and video devices could be incorporated into a LAN:

- Separate channels distinct from the digital data channels will be used.
- Data that is presented to the user in analog form will be transmitted in digital form on the LAN, with closed-circuit TV being a possible exception.
- Because of differing reliability and delay requirements, protocols somewhat different from those used for digital data will be needed to support voice and video devices (e.g., current work in this area includes the ARPANET Network Voice Protocol and the Internet protocol extensions such as the Internet Stream Protocol).

Provisions should be made in the LAN architecture to take advantage of the technical advances in the transmission of imagery. There will be increasing usage of communicating laser printers to serve high-speed image transmitters and receivers. The data rate required to support a laser printer is 256 Kbps.

Gateways

Requirements may exist for interconnecting the LAN with other data networks. The LAN should be able to support internetworking through one or more attached gate-

System Name	A/C Area	# CPU LAN/Serv Wide	# Terminals Service Wide	# Terminals LAN	Type Asynch/Synch	# Printer LAN	Codes ASCII/EBDIC	Other
1. Automated record control schedules		3/0	20	5	ASYNCH	3	ASCII	CP/M
2. Mail tracking system		2/0		240	SYNCH	60*	ASCII	WANG
3. Human resources network		3/2	70	2	ASYNCH	22	ASCII	UNIVAC UDLC
4. Management information system		2/0	106	13	ASYNCH	12		ZILOG
5. Labor relations information		20/0	10	3	ASYNCH	52	ASCII	
6. Office automation		0/1	60	210	SYNCH	22	ASCII	
7. Payroll/personnel		0/1	270	23	SYNCH/ASYNCH	2	ASCII	
8. Work planning and control system		2/5	25	10	ASYNCH	6	ASCII	

Figure 4-4 Digital Device Summary

*Est. 1 Printer for 4 Terminals

Network Traffic

way devices. Local network connections to public data networks would use gateway devices with local network protocols on one side and protocols, which are dependent on the transmission media, on the other side.

Security

Network security becomes a requirement when multiple user groups access the network and the information maintained by each group must be kept from other users. The network should be kept safe from unauthorized access attempts. As a minimum, the network security capability should include

- Limited physical access
- User authentication and password access mechanisms
- Traffic and message control
- File protection

The application is the driving factor in the determination of the degree of security required. A desirable requirement may be network controllable encryption devices independent of the host or terminal.

NETWORK TRAFFIC

Information Transmission

The LAN should support multiple information distribution channels. Information sources may be either analog or digital. Integration of these heterogeneous traffic types is desirable for economic reasons and for operational simplicity. The types of information transmission the LAN may need to support—digital data, voice, video, and imagery—are described below.

Digital Data. Digital data may pass between the communicating host digital processors, the communication gateways, and user terminal/workstations. These data are characterized as

- Interactive: These message transfers are generally short transactions of a few thousand bytes or less. Applications include terminal-to-host, terminal-to-terminal, and terminal-to-gateway (distant host interactions).
- Batch: This includes file transfers and other stream traffic. Applications include data base processing and archiving, and interprocess communication between hosts.

Figure 4-5, an example of a LAN digital data summary, provides a description of the digital data anticipated for the LAN systems designated for the sample LAN. This information was compiled from existing documentation and personnel inter-

System Name	Link Protocol	Average Message Length	Batch/ Interactive	Communications Rate	Security Requirements	Average Throughput			
						Day (Mbps)	Hour (Kbps)	Second bps	Peak bps
1. Automated record control schedules		4K Bytes	Interactive	4800	Medium	81.82	145248	2872	7053
2. Mail tracking system						4.58	560	160	590
3. Human resources network			Both	1200	Medium	160	20000	5565	13888
4. Management info. system		4K Bytes	Interactive	9600	Medium	39.9	4987	1385	3468
5. Labor relations information			Both	19,200	Medium	200	25000	7000	17360
6. Office automation system			Both	4800	Medium	1200	15000	41666	104166
7. Payroll/ personnel system		4K Bytes	Interactive	4800/9600	High	146	18250	5090	12725
8. Work, planning and central system			Both	9600 1200	Medium	166	20750	5763	14410

Figure 4-5 Digital Data Summary

Network Traffic

views. The information is not presented as a system requirement, but rather as a background reference for the overall LAN design.

Voice. The LAN may be required to support voice communications, even though applicational requirements may not be defined at the time of the study. Applications might range from intercom-like systems to a sophisticated network process that synchronizes voice, video, and data for teleconferencing applications.

Real-time digitized voice transmission on the LAN will require low delay and in-sequence delivery; however, the reliability requirements are less demanding than for digital data, because information quality is not significantly degraded by small data losses or errors.

Video. A desirable feature for the LAN would be the ability to support video data transmission. The video information can be digitized or, if the LAN provides analog as well as digital channels, the unprocessed video signal can be transmitted.

Digitized video would require extremely high data rates. Compression of the video image is a possible technique for reducing these. Also required for video transmission is a connection-oriented protocol with different quality-of-service parameters (flow and error control) than for digital data. Absolute reliability for digitized video is not essential because of redundancies of information content.

Imagery. This category includes facsimile, slow scan video, and raster graphics. The bandwidth necessary to support image transmission may be substantial, but the delay requirements are not normally as strict as for video or voice. Reliability requirements are not as strict as those for digital data in terminal traffic or file transfer applications because of informational redundancies.

Traffic Characteristics

The expected volume and statistical characteristics of traffic on the LAN affect many aspects of design. Information about the following is necessary:

- Traffic throughput
- Traffic classes (stream and transaction)
- Tolerable network delays
- Interconnectivity among nodes
- Concurrency of connections

Throughput Requirements. The LAN throughput requirement is a function of the capacity required of the transmission medium plus the processing capacity at each network node. Figure 4-6 is a representative sample of a throughput analysis. A quantitative analysis of all intended LAN applications should be accomplished.

System	Daily (Mbits)	Hourly (Kbits)	Bits Per Second	PEAK (bps)
Automated record control schedules	81.82	145248	2872	7053
Mail tracking system	4.58	560	160	590
Human resources network	160	20000	5565	13888
Management information system	39.9	4987	1385	3468
Labor relations information system	200	25000	7000	17360
Office automation	1200	15000	41666	104166
Payroll/personnel system	146	18250	5090	12725
Work planning and control system	166	20750	5763	14410
Totals	1998.30	249795	69501	173660

Figure 4-6 Average Traffic Throughput

Estimates should be made to determine

- Message sizes (peak, average, and variances)
- Responsiveness characteristics and requirements
- Interval between messages (peak, average, and variances)

Traffic Classes. It is desirable that a LAN support both connection-oriented (stream) and connectionless (datagram) classes of traffic. With a connection-oriented service, the network provides for the establishment of virtual connections over which data may be transferred, with the network providing error, sequence, and flow control. With a connectionless service, the network ensures that a received data unit contains no errors, but does not guarantee the delivery of every data unit submitted for transmission.

Most LAN applications require a connectionless service. This will be even more the case as terminals become smarter and less dependent upon hosts. Connection-oriented service is needed for applications such as file transfers to and from a local word processing workstation, or bulk data transfers between processes residing on different host processors. Nondigital (voice and video) stream traffic also requires connection-oriented transport services.

Tolerable Network Delay. Another LAN parameter is the network-induced delay that can be tolerated by the various applications. Requirements can be expressed in terms of absolute delay (maximum allowable delay experienced during transport) and delay variance (the maximum allowable delay variation within a data stream).

Network Traffic

Most of the network-induced delay in a LAN results from protocol processing. Since there is a trade-off between reliability (achieved by error detecting and correcting protocols) and delay (the performance penalty extracted by protocol processing), a compromise has to be made on an application basis. Inadequate processing power within the LAN nodes will lead to bottlenecks within the network itself.

There are three categories with respect to absolute delay requirements:

- *Real-time applications*—These applications cannot perform their function if network delay exceeds a certain value.

- *Applications that can tolerate some delay*—This includes interactive applications involving user terminals, where user satisfaction drops when delays increase above very small values. Most applications will fall into this category. For interactive applications, delay should not exceed two seconds. Delays induced by the LAN should not exceed two seconds. Delays resulting from other factors (e.g., terminal type, inquiry type, data rate) may cause delays to exceed two seconds for certain applications. Figure 4-7 illustrates required response times as a function of user activity.

- *Applications that are relatively insensitive to network delay*—This includes batch processing, file transfer, and electronic mail applications.

User activity	"Maximum" response time
System activation (system initialization)	3.0 seconds
Error feedback	2-4
Response to ID	2.0
Keyboard entry	0.1
Information on next procedure	5.0
Response to simple inquiry	2.0
Response to complex inquiry	2-4
Request for next page	0.5-1
Response to "execute problem"	15.0
Response to graphic manipulation	2-4

Figure 4-7 System Response Time

Benchmark Model. As described in Chapter 3, Model Approach to Local Area Network Design, the model should include the data rates (average and peak) and other traffic characteristics (such as stream or transaction traffic). This benchmark model is needed to determine protocol processing capabilities required and the adequacy of various LAN topologies in terms of throughput, channel utilization, and system delays.

A network administrator can use the model to analyze various "what if" situations, such as the addition of high data rate modems or new channel allocations.

Network Traffic Summary

The types of traffic—digital data, voice, video, and imagery—that may be transmitted on the LAN place two major requirements on network services: (1) transmission rates must be adequate for each information type, and (2) protocols appropriate to each information type must be defined and provided.

RELIABILITY

Level of Reliability/Availability

Reliability requirements are application-specific, and the networkwide reliability requirement will be the requirement of its most critical application. In addition to the hardware reliability, there are transmission reliability requirements for each application that are affected by the protocols employed. Different classes of traffic, such as stream (e.g., file transfers), interactive voice, and video, have different reliability requirements. For instance, file transfers must be reliable with respect to delivery, data sequence, and bit errors, whereas voice applications require sequencing, but some data loss or some bit errors are not critical.

Another factor affecting availability is the sizing of the LAN. If the LAN or any of its nodes becomes significantly overburdened for more than very brief periods, effective availability is reduced.

Redundancy

High LAN reliability and availability requirements must be translated into redundancy requirements for the LAN components. Redundancy requirements differ, depending on the type of transmission medium and access methodology employed by the LAN component. For instance, most twisted pair PBX LANs utilize a central switching computer for transmission routings. Because of its star topology, if the central switch fails, the entire network fails. Thus, some form of redundancy would be required for the central switch. Analysis of component failure and the effect on the various LAN assemblies will determine the redundancy requirements. Many baseband networks use two cables, so that if one node fails, the network will continue to operate.

Node or Link Failure

An analysis should be made of the consequences of network node or link failures. Two areas need to be addressed once the system has been selected: (1) identification of the critical elements of the system, and (2) maximum allowable time and frequency of outages that can be tolerated on a system-by-system basis. Network links can be classified according to their importance to the network or to some particular application. Toleration of failure and frequency of failure can also be determined on a per-application basis. This should be part of an ongoing network management program.

Error Control

In reference to the ISO model, basic error control procedures are implemented at the link layer and continue up to the application layer. Generally the degree of error control provided is a function of the protocol being used. A connection-oriented transport protocol will generally provide delivery, bit, and sequence error control, whereas a network-layer datagram protocol may not guarantee bit reliability. Upon detection of an error, the network will retransmit the data in an attempt to correct the invalid data. As a minimum, the network should provide end-to-end digital data transmission with a bit error rate (BER) of less than 10^{-9}. This is required to support the most stringent requirement necessary for digital data bulk transfers. (Reference: *The Selection of Local Area Computer Networks*, NBS Special Publication 500-96, U.S. Department of Commerce, November 1982.)

GROWTH REQUIREMENTS

The data-communications environment is dynamic and the network that is required to support data communications must be capable of meeting these changing needs. The physical network should have a life cycle of over 10 years, whereas the message network may have a life cycle of less than five years.

Additional Nodes

The LAN architecture should be configured so that the addition of new nodes to the network can be implemented with little impact to the existing network. A minimum five-year life cycle should be planned.

Traffic Increases and Changes

As the life cycle of the LAN progresses, traffic characteristics may change, reflecting modifications in network operations. For example, the initial teleconferencing requirements may be expected to be very low, but as applications develop, they may require a large percentage of the available bandwidth. The network should have the flexibility to handle traffic and protocol changes with minimum impact on the existing system.

Internetworking Requirements

The LAN should have the capability for communication access to other networks as applications require. Factors to be considered for internetworking requirements include

- Internetwork protocols
- Type of service
- Gateway medium

- Access methods
- Data rates
- Data units
- Addressing methods

The National Bureau of Standards is presently developing internetworking standards which are fully compatible with the work of the IEEE 802 committee on LANs. Because LANs are a developing technology, one of the driving forces that must be considered is the vendor-dependent available gateway devices.

Equipment Reconfigurations

Considering the dynamic environment of most organizations, it may become necessary to move equipment between offices and buildings. The LAN should have the flexibility for inexpensive and easy equipment reconfigurations.

NETWORK ADMINISTRATION

This section describes the information-gathering functions needed to manage a distributed LAN environment. The information collected may be viewed from different perspectives for various management purposes. Network management and control mechanisms will be required for configuration control, maintenance, security, and accounting purposes.

Network Monitoring

Some of the administrative information to be monitored and collected by the network may include

- Distributions
  - Packet size
  - Packet type
  - Packet arrival times
- Sources of delay
  - Channel acquisition
  - Communication (LAN) delay
- Successful and unsuccessful transmission
  - Collision counts
  - Retry counts
- Communication matrices
  - Terminal-to-host
  - Host-to-host
  - Terminal-to-gateway
  - Host-to-gateway

Network Administration

- Throughput and utilization
  - Physical medium bandwidth
  - Nodal resources (processor and memory utilization, buffer queue lengths)
  - Protocol processing measurements
  - Error reporting
- Equipment status
  - Frequency of use
  - Operational status
  - Line status

Many of the statistics mentioned above will be useful in developing and defining the network traffic workload characterization. The workload characterization will aid short-term performance monitoring and tuning and long-range capacity planning. The LAN performance monitoring will also require detailed analysis of protocol processing times and other potential sources of delay.

Problems such as increasing traffic demands will require the development of capacity-planning techniques. LAN utilization productivity and responsiveness indices will provide top-level management with a quantitative viewpoint on the LAN performance and allow long-range trends in usage to be understood. The benchmark model will be useful in developing "what if" situations in regard to long-range planning.

Network Control

Network control can be very sophisticated and will become even more so with the continued vendor competition for new products. Most network control functions can be classified as "desirable" rather than mandatory requirements. Some of these items are

- NIU Assignment
  - A user can select his or her own call number, have it verified by the controller and inserted into a look-up table, or the controller can assign a call number to a new user.
  - A controller can, upon query from a terminal, look for a specific host on the same channel, another channel, or another LAN, and provide the identification interface to the terminal and host.
- NIU Data Rates
  - A controller can remotely adjust data rates on the NIU based upon rate of data to be transmitted or received.
- Encryption
  - A key distribution center can be used to establish encryption between two or more consenting nodes.
- Configuration
  - Perhaps the most basic use of network management is to maintain configura-

tion control. Tables and libraries are maintained concerning node addresses, data rates, and other pertinent information.

Maintenance

The individual hardware and software components of the network must be maintained. For hardware, this generally means preventive and corrective maintenance to ensure a working system. Software maintenance generally implies changes to the software to enhance or modify a network function.

One problem of a complex hardware and software system such as a local area network is the determination of which component or combination of components is responsible for network failure. Often it is difficult to determine whether the network failure resulted from a hardware or a software malfunction. Thus the maintenance of network hardware cannot be performed in isolation from the maintenance of network software. Network maintenance operations should include the following functions:

- Monitoring network status
  — Real-time displays of node and link status
  — Maintenance of historical logs to analyze recurring problems
  — Automatic failure detection of critical system elements
  — Artificial traffic generation to probe element status or exercise specific network functions
  — Frequency-response monitoring of analog LAN components
- Providing first-level maintenance support, including preventive maintenance, failed component replacement and simple fixes, and modification.
- Implementing hardware and software configuration controls

Hardware. Maintenance of the network hardware can be considered from two perspectives: (1) periodic preventive maintenance, and (2) correction and recovery from failure. The division of maintenance responsibility is generally structured along these lines, with periodic preventive maintenance done in-house and corrective maintenance contracted outside if the network fails. There are both advantages and disadvantages to this approach: trade-offs can be used to determine the most advantageous method, dependent upon the system selected.

Another factor affecting hardware maintenance is compatibility with established standards. As the network market evolves and matures, and as national and international standards are adopted, equipment will become more standardized. There will be less vendor-custom-manufactured equipment, and the benefits from off-the-shelf, vendor-independent components can be utilized. The advantages of a vendor-independent system from the viewpoint of maintenance include

- The ability to choose equipment for maintenance reasons (e.g., good vendor service reputation)

Network Administration

- The ability to drop a vendor if a poor maintenance record is established

Software. When specialized network capabilities are required, it is necessary for either the network vendor or in-house personnel to develop nonstandard software. Inclusion of such specialized software affects maintenance. Factors affecting the maintenance of custom software include

- Modularity of design
- Use of accepted programming practices such as structured programming techniques
- Quality of documentation

As with custom hardware, the benefits anticipated from the use of custom software should be weighed carefully against the potential problems of maintaining the software. All software should be developed in accordance with Federal Information Processing Standards (FIPS).

Depending on the technical sophistication of the installation's staff, software maintenance can be performed in-house or contracted out to the network vendor or a third party. The potential advantages of in-house software maintenance include

- Quick response to problems
- Administrative control over individual maintenance decisions
- Enhanced technical control over total network functions
- Reduced total maintenance costs

In-house software maintenance can be cost-effective with sufficient staffing and if the software is carefully documented. If these criteria are not met, in-house software maintenance can lead to exploding costs and system deterioration. Often simple software modifications affect other functions in unexpected ways. On the other hand, if the software was originally developed in-house, then in-house maintenance is more likely to be cost effective.

During network procurement, the costs of outside software maintenance and the costs of unscheduled network outages must be weighed against the costs of in-house software maintenance to determine the installation's maintenance requirements.

5

Alternative Technologies

This chapter presents simplified design layouts for four alternative approaches for fulfilling the requirements discussed in Chapter 4. For each alternative approach, the major features discussed are based on the capacities or limitations of a specific manufacturer's system. A specific product was actually selected in order to provide realistic designs and cost figures; however, the manufacturers are identified only as Companies X, Y, and Z in this book.

As you will recall, our example in Chapter 4 refers to three multistoried buildings, with the main building constructed around four large light courts. All cables must be distributed through the corridors. In addition, an arcade and a driveway impede cable paths on the first two floors, making it necessary to route the cables up to the third floor before the break for the arcade and then down to the offices on the second and first floor levels of the sections past the arcade. A similar situation exists at the other buildings, which have arcades and open driveways. All alternative approaches discussed in the following sections will be based on the same cable routing, which takes these factors into consideration.

ALTERNATIVE #1 — PRIVATE BRANCH EXCHANGE

The digital private branch exchange (PBX) is a switching device that ties telephones, data and word processing, facsimile, and even slow-scan video equipment into private or public networks. Until recently, PBXs were used primarily to make voice transmission cost-effective by packing a large number of calls into a small number of lines. Newer generations of PBXs are being designed to handle data rates of up to 10 MHz.

Alternative #1—Private Branch Exchange   43

Many PBXs are being designed to interact with LANs. A PBX can interface with a LAN in one of three ways: (1) through an independent gateway which performs the necessary protocol and format conversions; (2) through the purchase of a compatible PBX and LAN, typically from the same vendor; or (3) through the purchase of digital PBXs that have X.25 gateways incorporated into their switches, making them compatible with packetized, X.25 compatible LANs.

Device Interface

A possible design of a PBX system for our example would be configured as shown in Figure 5-1.

This design is based upon the equipment of Company X. The main switch and control station for the PBX could be located on any floor. The connectivity to the offices on all floors is via multiple two-pair cables with a two-pair telephone cable dedicated to each data and voice station.

There are approximately 250 offices per floor in our example. We are making an assumption that there will be an average of two data terminals per office. In order to minimize the amount of cabling, the proposed design utilizes multiplexers to combine all data signals for a floor into two multiplexers. The connectivity from each multiplexer to the main switch is a serial data stream via coaxial cable.

This connectivity is defined as a multiple star topology with each multiplexer as the central node of its own star. In turn, each multiplexer is connected to the main switching unit which serves as the central node of the master star. Company X has designed its system with redundancy in multiplexers and in the master switch in order to reduce the probability of a loss of access, for large numbers of users, due to system failure. The redundant components and connectivity are illustrated in Figure 5-2. Each interface multiplexer (IM) consists of redundant processors which control access of up to 256 integrated terminal equipment (ITE) or data auxiliary units. The ITE is an electronic telephone unit with data interface capability. Data auxiliary units contain special controllers: packet controllers, modem interface cards, or data access boards.

Each ITE voice and data terminal may interface with voice and a data device simultaneously. The data device may operate at a bit rate of up to 56 Kbps, and voice is in digital format at 64 Kbps.

Connectivity from the ITEs to the IM is accomplished by the use of a two-pair standard telephone cable. Each IM will provide electronic switch selection of up to 256 ITE ports. There will be two multiplexers on each floor of the main building; therefore, there will be up to 500 two-pair cables at the point of interconnect with the IMs.

Each IM has redundant coaxial cables which connect it to the centrally located Main Control Unit (MCU). Colocated with the MCU are switch network (SN) modules which perform the main switching function for the system. There is an SN module associated with each cable from an IM. Switching network groups are formed by combining eight SN module pairs. An SN module pair consists of SNs A and B. SN

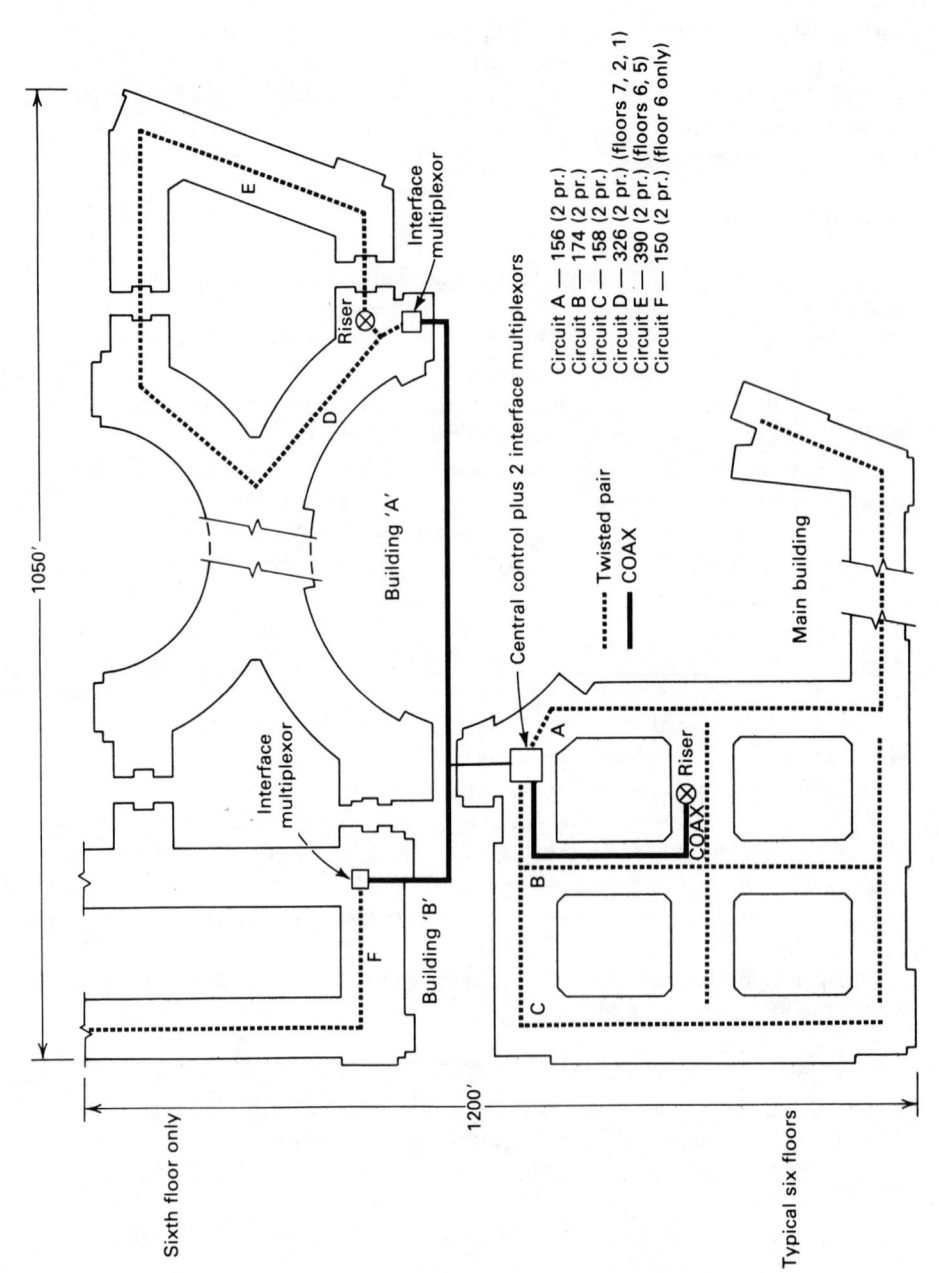

Figure 5-1 Digital PBX System Typical Floor Layout

Circuit A — 156 (2 pr.)
Circuit B — 174 (2 pr.)
Circuit C — 158 (2 pr.)
Circuit D — 326 (2 pr.) (floors 7, 2, 1)
Circuit E — 390 (2 pr.) (floors 6, 5)
Circuit F — 150 (2 pr.) (floor 6 only)

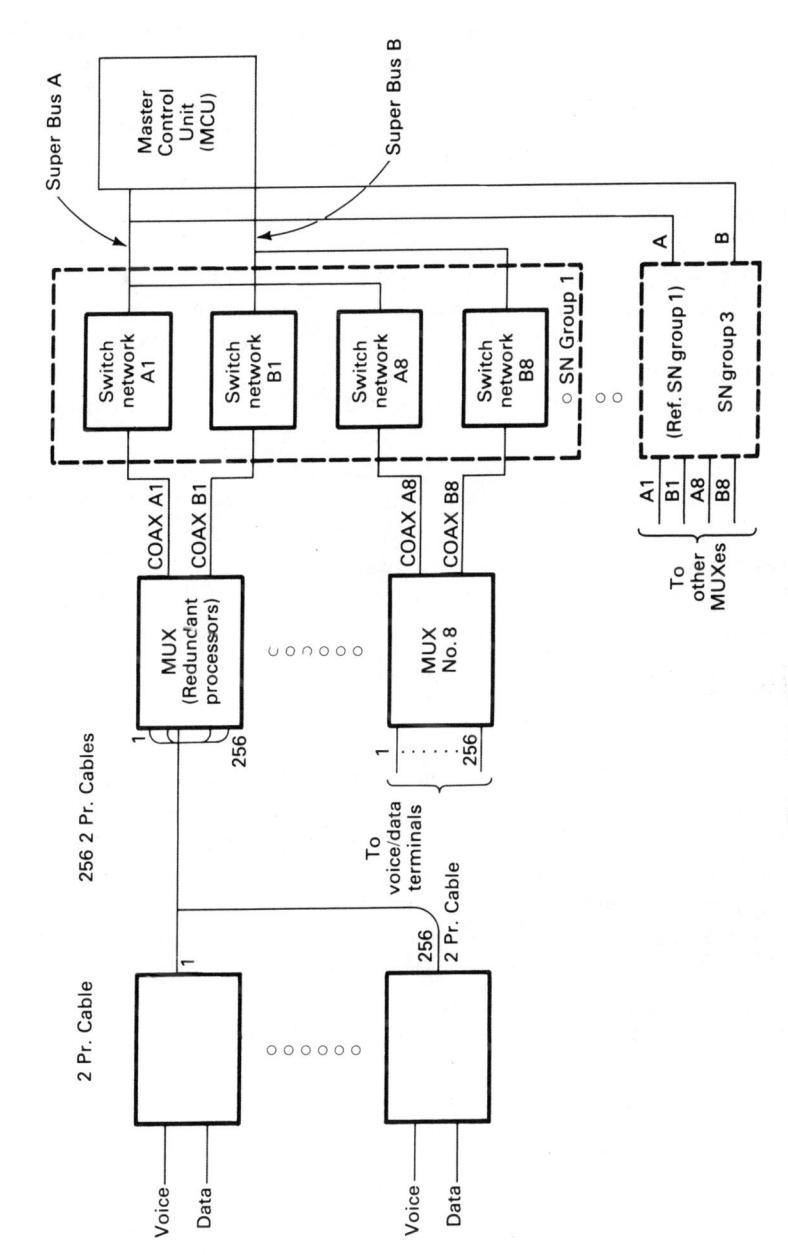

Figure 5-2 Typical PBX Configuration

groups are connected to the A and B modules of two other SN groups to form super buses A and B which are controlled by processors A and B of the MCU respectively. Therefore the connectivity is fully redundant for each IM. This redundancy means that a failure will affect a maximum of 16 voice and data ports.

Network Communications Flow

The maximum data rate of each individual data phone is 56 Kbps, which can be handled simultaneously with digitized voice at a rate of 64 Kbps. The multiplexer has a maximum capacity of 256 ports and a maximum data rate of 41.4 Mbps to the master switch. Therefore, the multiplexer has the capacity to handle a total of 512 voice and data lines. In the main building there will be two multiplexers required per floor to handle 500 data terminals. The combined data stream out of each multiplexer is interfaced to the main control unit via a switching unit. There will be 24 multiplexers and switching units in the system.

The numbers given only take into consideration the data terminals in the system, but the PBX is primarily a voice switching system and there is a total requirement to interface 6000 telephones, including those with and without data capability.

Multiplexers will be used to interface with the world outside via common carrier trunks. This PBX configuration is a way to enable intercommunications among any of the data users via the data switching capabilities of the system.

ALTERNATIVE #2 — BASEBAND

A baseband LAN uses a cable media, usually coaxial but sometimes twisted pair, for communications between nodes at the data rates of the user equipment. Through the technique of time-division multiplexing of multiple data signals to form a single-composite data stream at a higher data rate, many terminals may simultaneously communicate with each other. The number of simultaneous communication exchanges which may take place is a function of the total bandwidth of the communications media and the aggregate bandwidth required for the user terminals. A typical baseband system operates at a bit rate of 10 Mbps, which is a limiting factor for the number of simultaneous users which may be accommodated. Typically, a baseband network will be limited to less than 1000 users.

It is possible to connect more than one baseband network, using gateways between the networks. To communicate with outside users, standard modems connected to common carrier lines may be used. The interface between the modem and the NIU port will be a standard RS–232C interconnect using ASCII formatted data and asynchronous communications. The baseband network by Company Y is the product which has been used to describe this alternative. Company Y uses ring topology and token passing for access control. Figure 5-3 illustrates the concept, using ten separate ring networks with a central ring as a hub in the case of inter-ring communications.

The Company Y system uses dual coaxial cables to form a dual ring system.

Alternative #2—Baseband

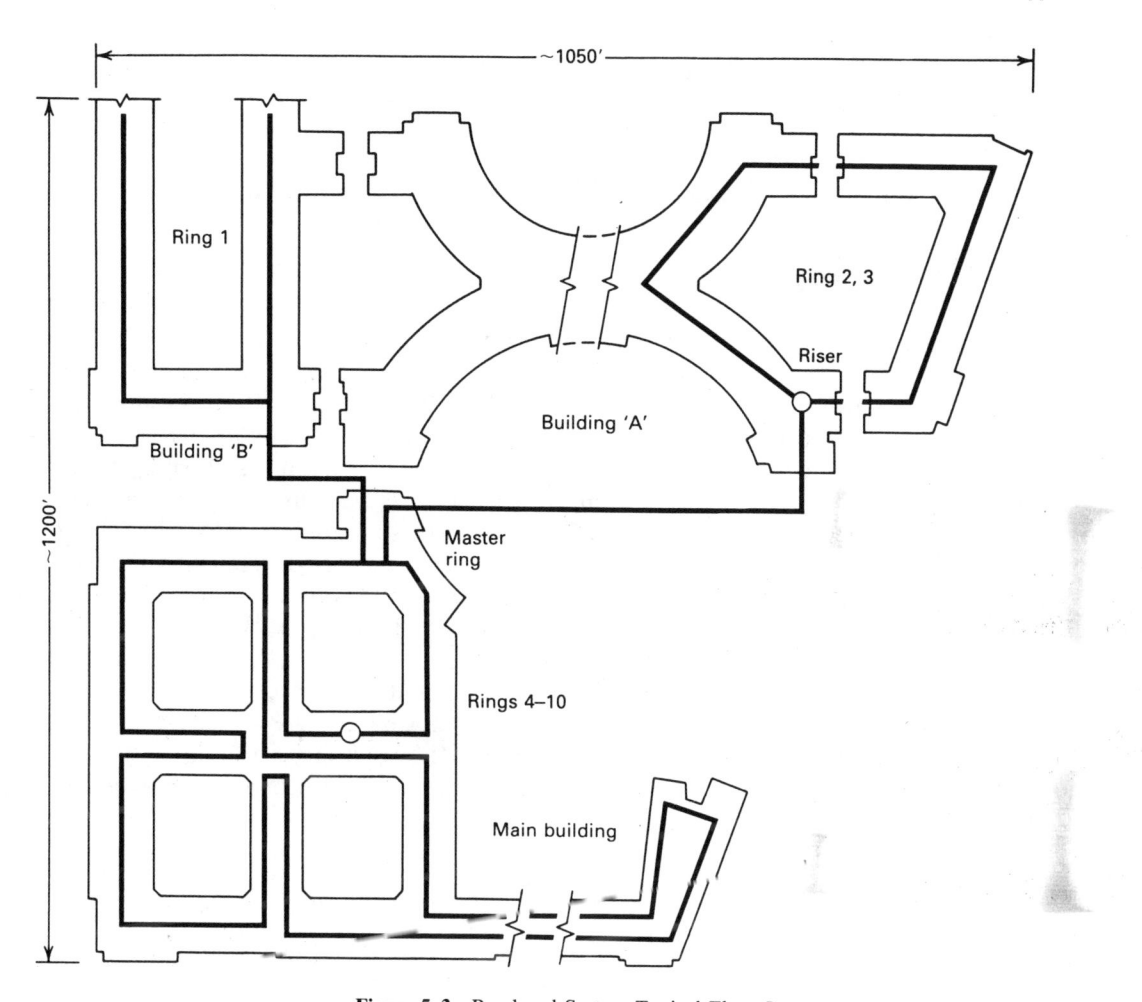

Figure 5-3 Baseband System Typical Floor Layout

Each ring has a director: a microprocessor-controller which generates packets and circulates them around the network. The director also controls the number of packets on the network at any time to maintain a throughput of more than 3 Mbps. Each packet contains a token field which is examined by the interface device of each node around the ring. The token may be in one of two states. One state indicates that there is "data present" in the packet; the second state indicates "no data." The packet also contains addresses for the source and destination nodes, so that each interface device examines the address of every packet with a "data present" token for its own address. If there is an address match, the interface device accepts the data from the information field and changes the token to "no data" status. This packet now becomes available for use.

With the multiple ring concept, the center ring is located on the fourth floor of the main building. In addition, there is a ring dedicated to each remaining floor in the main building and in the nearby buildings. The center ring services all equipment on the fourth floor in addition to the gateways to all other rings. This connectivity allows communications between any two rings with minimum delay and the least interaction of intermediate rings.

Network Access

The interface of any user device to the LAN is accomplished through the use of two elements of the system (see Figure 5-4). The direct connection to the dual coaxial cable is made with a cable access point (CAP). The CAP is connected via a multiconductor cable to a terminal access point (TAP). Each TAP has two ports for user devices. The TAP is a microprocessor-controlled device which may be programmed to adjust data parameters and formats. The two ports are individually programmable to allow devices of different characteristics to be supported.

The CAP is a passive circuit that provides the means of tapping into the network. A CAP does not require a device to be connected on the user side; therefore, it is good practice in the initial network layout to locate CAPs wherever a need to add a user device at some later time is anticipated. Adding to the network then becomes a simple matter of connecting the TAP and user devices.

The network has a maximum capacity per ring of 250 TAPs, which is equivalent to 500 devices. All interfaces to the TAP on the device side must conform to RS-232C, but the TAP will operate with both asynchronous and synchronous data at rates up to 19.2 Kbps.

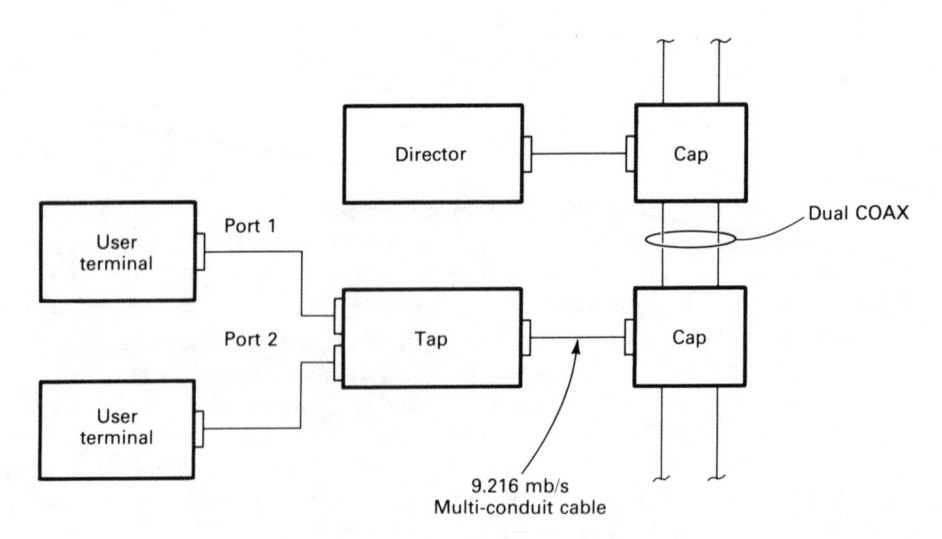

Figure 5-4 Baseband Interface Components

Alternative #2—Baseband

Network Communications Flow

The flow of packets around a ring is controlled by the director for the ring. Several fields of each packet are used by TAPs around the ring and by the director to send and receive data, acknowledge receipt, and assure that no occupied packet makes the trip around the ring more than once. The packet-header bits change during these transactions as illustrated in Figure 5-5. The figure only provides an example of how these bits change state, it does not show an exact configuration of the packet bits. As indicated, the packet has all of the bits set to zero when it is generated by the director and inserted into the data stream on the network cable. When TAP #1 has data to send to TAP #3, it captures the packet. In step 2, TAP #1 inserts data into the packet, sets the token and monitor bits of the packet, and sets the address to 3 (binary 11). The occupied packet is sent to TAP #2, which forwards it without change to TAP #3. When TAP #3 recognizes its address, it captures the data from the data field and sets the acknowledge bit. In step 3, the director receives the occupied packet and resets the monitor bit. When TAP #1 (the source of the data) receives the packet, it resets the token and acknowledge bits, clearing the packet for further use.

Network Reliability

The dual ring topology of the Company Y system provides the means for "self-healing" in the event of a failure. The self-healing takes place when a TAP attempts to send a packet forward and detects that there is a failure between it and the next TAP. The signal is then looped around via the directors on each side of the cable break. The detected cable break or equipment failure is recorded on the logging printer as an indication that maintenance is required.

DESCRIPTION	ADDRESS	TOKEN	MONITOR	ACKNOWLEDGE
STEP 1: Empty packet generated by director	00	0	0	0
STEP 2: Tap #1 inserts data, sets token & address, monitor	11	1	1	0
STEP 3: Tap #2 Passes packet on	11	1	1	0
STEP 4: Tap #3 Acknowledges data	11	1	1	1
STEP 5: Director resets monitor	11	1	0	1
STEP 6: Tap #1 Reset	00	0	0	0

Figure 5-5 Packet Header Bits Change

ALTERNATIVE #3 — BROADBAND

The broadband LAN concept uses a combination of two technologies: cable television networks and computers. The merger of these technologies has resulted in a means of networking large numbers of terminals along with multiple CPUs and special-purpose user devices. The concept makes use of the radio frequency spectrum between 5 and 400 MHz as a carrier for information at data rates up to the multimegabit range, which includes the capacity for real-time video channels. The broad spectrum available in this range provides a means of communication between electronic data devices presently available or likely to be developed in the immediate future.

The diagram in Figure 5-6 illustrates the connectivity of a typical broadband LAN. This diagram represents a mid-split system with a transmit frequency range of 100–140 MHz and a receive frequency range of 160–200 MHz. Data flows bidirectionally on the trunk cable. Transmitted data from a device interface (DI) is converted to a frequency shift key (FSK) signal in a frequency band within the transmit range indicated. The FSK signal is converted to the receive-frequency band by the frequency converter and is frequency-division multiplexed (FDM) by the bandpass filter.

The translated carrier is FSK-modulated by the data in a frequency band within the receive range, detected by the destination DI, and received by the destination user device. It is a common practice in the design of broadband LANs to assign many devices to a single transmit-receive channel pair, allowing direct communications between all devices on the channel pair. A channel pair may have a bandwidth of up to 10 MHz, depending upon the system design chosen.

Channel access is on a demand basis; therefore, it is possible to have a conflict when more than one device attempts to send messages simultaneously. To handle conflicts, the CSMA/CD technique is used by many vendors.

Device Interface

For the purpose of this discussion, the broadband LAN will be based upon Company Z's network design. The overall layout of a typical floor is shown in Figure 5-7. The headend equipment for the entire network of the three-building complex is located on the sixth floor of the main building. From the headend, the trunk cable is routed to the cable riser for the building. At the basement level the trunk cable is routed under the street to the other buildings.

Each user device to be interfaced with the network must be both electrically and functionally connected through a network interface unit (NIU). To communicate with outside users, standard modems, connected to common carrier lines, may be used. The interface between the modem and the NIU port will be a standard RS-232C interconnect using ASCII-formatted data and asynchronous communications. Each NIU has six ports and will support six user devices. The location of the NIUs should be carefully selected in order to optimize the lengths of cables required to connect to the NIUs. This cable length is important from a cost standpoint, since trunk cable is more expensive than standard coaxial drop cable or distribution cable.

Alternative #3—Broadband

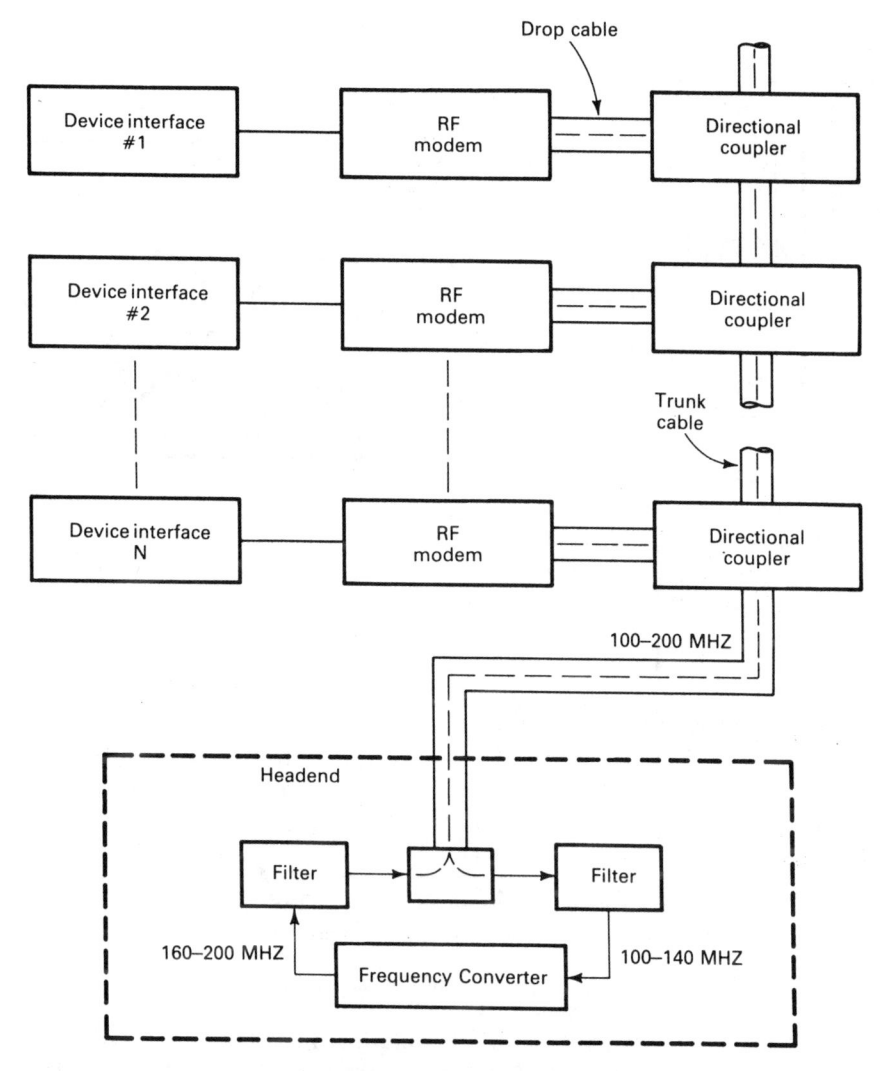

Figure 5-6 Simplified Diagram of a Broadband LAN

It is also important from a signal-level standpoint, since standard coaxial cable has more loss than trunk cable.

The NIU microprocessor is controlled to act as an independent, intelligent network node. This intelligence involves several major functions: formatting data into packets, speed conversion, and routing data to specified destinations. For receiving data, the NIU manages all hand-shaking and conversion of packet data into device-compatible data. Each NIU executes software that coordinates its activities with the activities of other NIUs on the network. Thus, each NIU can participate in a variety of cooperative network operations, such as network configuration and con-

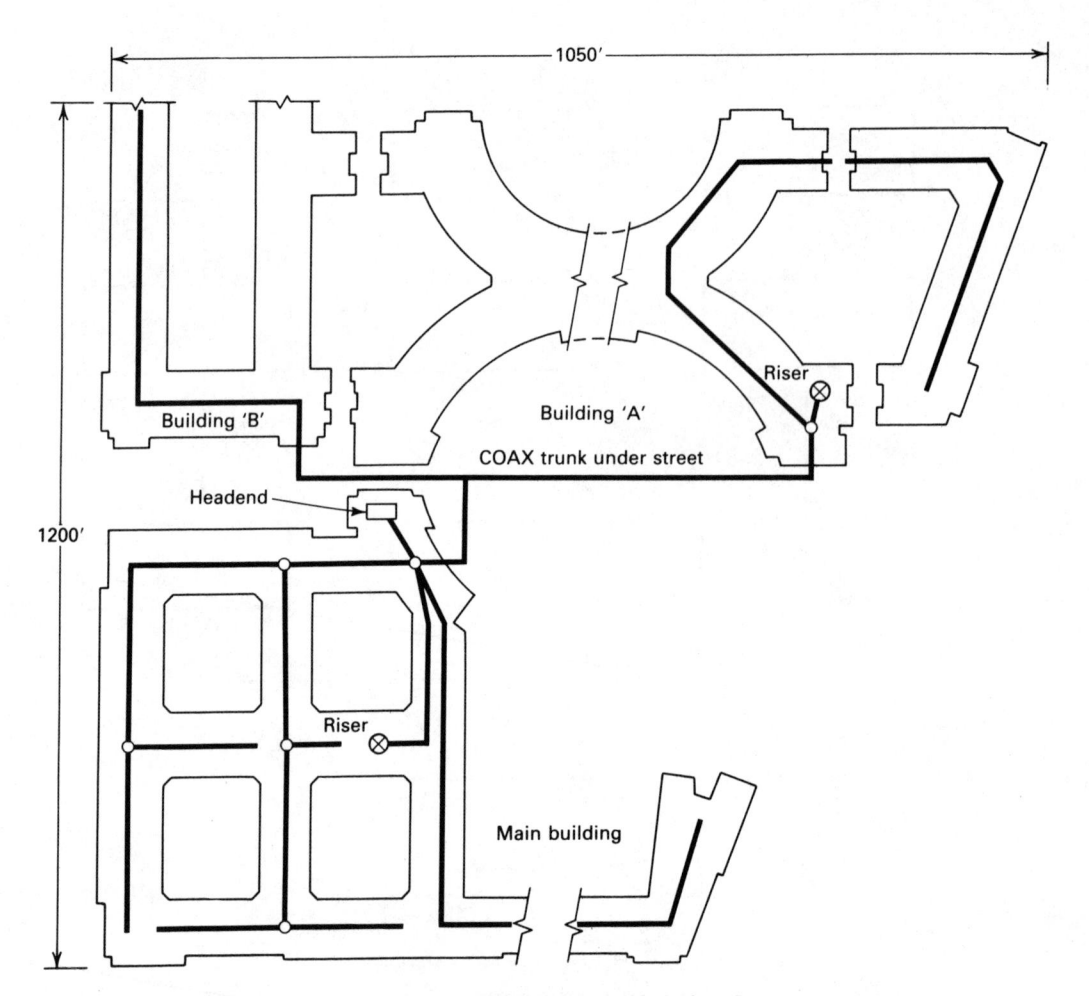

Figure 5-7 Broadband Typical Floor Layout

trol, fault isolation, and statistics acquisition. In addition, each NIU can execute diagnosis that isolate operating faults to the printed-circuit-board level. As shown in Figure 5-8, the packetized data interface between the NIU and the cable radio frequency (RF) modem is at a data rate of 5 Mbps. The RF modem to cable data is FSK-encoded in a standard RF channel pair of frequencies.

Radio Frequency Subsystem

The radio frequency subsystem includes the cable and all passive and active RF components. The detailed network design consists of selection of components which exhibit characteristics that allow end-to-end signal levels that are within the operational values of the active RF components. The active components consist of the RF modems, frequency translators, and amplifiers.

Alternative #3—Broadband

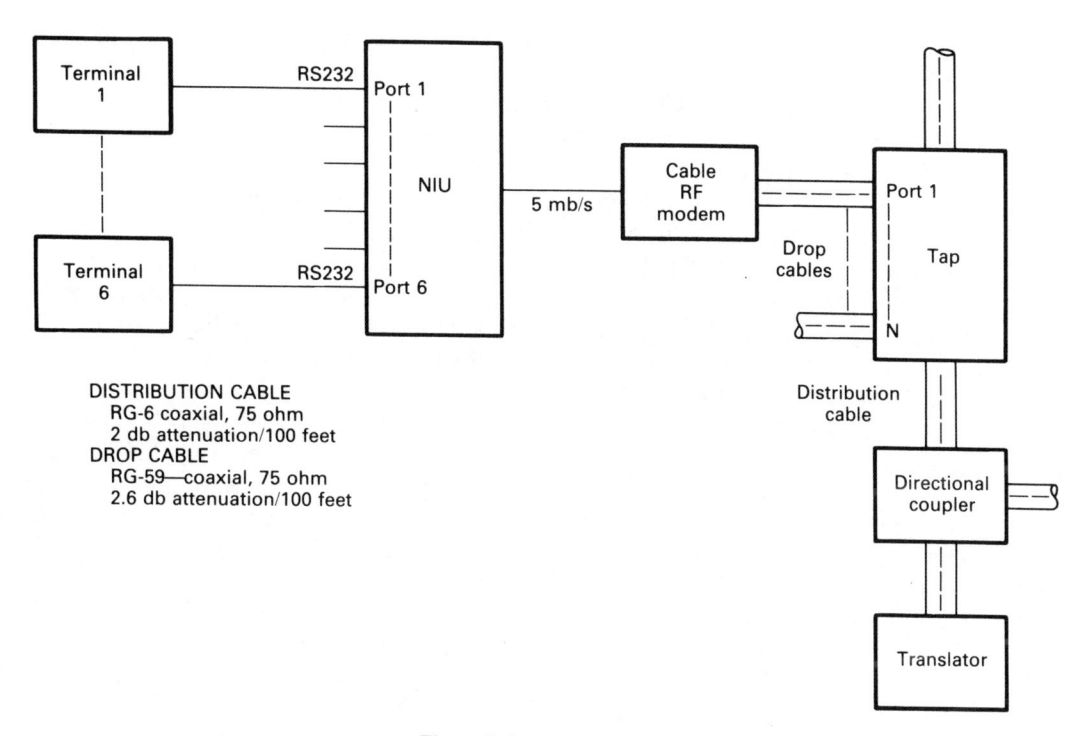

Figure 5-8 Packetized Data Interface

The active components are adjustable within a limited range; therefore, the installation process includes tuning of the network and verification by test that the predicted numbers are met. Some adjustable components must serve multiple paths, and adjustment of these components must be followed by a test of all affected nodes.

Network Communications Flow

Access to the network is controlled by the individual NIUs using the CSMA/CD approach. This concept was described earlier, in Chapter 2; however, the technique of implementing the concept will be discussed in some detail at this time.

Actual packet transmission is closely coordinated with receiver information. Before transmission, the receiver examines the network to determine whether the line is quiet. When the receiver senses network activity, transmission is delayed. When the network is available, the transmitter encodes the packet and shifts it on to the network via the transceiver. The receiver continues to monitor the network. When it detects invalid encoding (indicating that another NIU is attempting simultaneous transmission, or some other interference), it signals the transmitter that a collision has occurred.

If a number of nodes attempt to transmit at the same time, their attempts will overlap and intefere with one another, resulting in a "collision." A node can experience a collision during the initial part of its transmission attempt (known as the "collision window"), before its transmitted signal has had time to propagate to all parts of the network.

Once the collision window has passed, the node has acquired the network, and subsequent collisions should not happen. All other nodes should have noticed the signal (via carrier sense) and deferred to it. The time required to acquire the network is based on the round-trip propagation time of the coaxial cable.

In the event of a collision, the NIU notices the collision first, and turns on the collision detect signal. The NIU then "enforces" the collision by transmitting a bit sequence called the "jam." By "jamming" the network, the NIU makes the collision last long enough to be noticed by other transmitting nodes involved in the collision. After jamming the network, the NIU terminates the transmission and schedules a retransmission attempt after some random period of time. Retransmission is attempted repeatedly in the face of repeated collisions. Because repeated collisions indicate a busy net, the NIU voluntarily delays its own retransmissions to reduce its load on the net. This step is known as "backing off," and is accomplished by expanding the random retransmission interval selected on each retransmission attempt. The transmission eventually succeeds, or the NIU abandons the attempt on the assumption that the net has failed, or has become overloaded.

The receiving node(s) receive and decode the bits resulting from a collision just as if they were bits of a valid frame. Collisions do not turn on the receiving node's collision detect signal, which is generated only during transmission. Instead, fragmentary frames received during collisions are distinguished from valid frames by the NIU, by noting that a collision fragment is always smaller than the shortest valid frame. The NIU discards fragments shorter than the shortest valid frame.

Network Reliability

The components used in the network are all readily available, fully developed products. The NIUs are designed with integrated circuitry throughout and will have a mean time between failure (MTBF) in excess of 5000 hours. The RF subsystem components have MTBFs of over 100,000 hours (10 years). Also, the techniques used in data encoding along with error detection and automatic retransmission result in a system which is capable of moving data with low probability of error. The NIU-specified bit error rate is less than one error in 10^8 bits.

ALTERNATIVE #4—HYBRID

The hybrid approach to a LAN would consist of a broadband network in the main building and a baseband network in each of the other two buildings. The baseband and broadband portions would have the same characteristics as described previously. This approach would be an effective way to implement a phased system in which some of the offices would initially be provided with a networking capability only for standard microsystems and terminals at data rates at or below 19.2 Kbps. An additional advantage to this approach is that the protocol-transparent baseband system

Alternative #4 — Hybrid

could be used to interconnect nonstandard terminals with their host processors. This approach requires only that the terminal interface be electrically compatible with RS-232C. The broadband and baseband portions could be linked by installing cable under the street, so that in the future the broadband system could be expanded to include the offices in the other buildings. In the initial stages, however, the users at the adjacent buildings would have the capability to communicate with users in the main building. The interface between the dissimilar media would be established via a gateway. This approach would accommodate the implementation of an electronic mail system, but would not allow the use of high data rate equipment such as real-time video and high-speed graphics on the baseband portions of the network. It would not preclude the use of standard graphics, under 19.2 Kbps, or store-and-forward video. NIUs would be used to provide gateways to other networks as required.

6

Comparison of Alternatives

This chapter illustrates how alternative configuration designs can be evaluated by means of a modularized procedure and compared by using constant methodology. A similar approach is used in establishing evaluation weights. Should the reader desire to readjust the weighting factors for the evaluation criteria, additional analyses could be simply performed.

The basic assumption used in this comparison of alternatives is that all systems (proposed or to be proposed) meet the mandatory requirements, are capable of performing the desired objectives, and may or may not contain features in addition to these basic requirements.

EVALUATION CRITERIA

Various techniques for performing trade-off analyses were investigated in order to provide a measure of objectivity in the evaluation. The weighted matrices technique was selected because of its versatility and because it is more appropriate for evaluating systems where actual costs of attributes cannot be determined. Under this system the designer preassigns varying quantities of points to all network factors considered important. The system with the most points is then selected.

Because the assignment of points, or values, is subjective, there is likely to be a difference of scale factors and ratings among persons and organizations assigning the points. To reduce this subjectivity, let several engineers establish numerical ratings for each of the alternative designs, then average these ratings and round the number to the reflected accuracy. As an example, weighted ratings of 0.4, 0.6, 0.7, and 0.6 from four engineers would give a rating of 0.6, whereas inputs of 0.99, 0.98,

Life Cycle Cost Factors

Factors	Points
System availability and reliability	20
Response time	5
Growth capability	15
Training requirements and ease of operation	5
Compatibility and connectivity	10
Maintenance and logistics support	10
Security	5
Transition impact	15
Relative life cycle costs	15
Total	100

Figure 6-1 Weighted Matrices

0.95, and 0.98 would be recorded as 0.98. The weighted rating approach enables reevaluation of the decision at any time during the conceptual design. The reader can easily modify the weighted ratings should user requirements change.

An example of evaluation criteria and relative weights assigned to these criteria is shown in Figure 6-1.

The reader could select any number of criteria, but for a more manageable list it is best to have a maximum of 10 characteristics with a total value of 100 points. The weight to be placed on each criterion can then be assigned. Each of the four alternative system designs, or any other proposed design, can be rated using this methodology.

System Availability and Reliability is considered one of the more important criterion and includes hardware, software, and operational performance. Functional requirements for Response Time and for Growth Capability must be met by all proposed candidates, although individual response rates as well as capacity for growth may vary from candidate to candidate. Training Requirements and Ease of Operation are expected to be minimal for all candidates and ideally should be transparent to the user. Compatibility and Connectivity will vary with each proposed candidate, with some exhibiting more flexibility than others. Maintenance and Logistics Support would affect reliability, but is considered to be a separate characteristic.

All proposed candidates must meet the minimum functional Security requirements, although some candidates may provide a greater capability in this area. Transition Impact will vary between the proposed candidates, but can be minimized with proper management and scheduling. Life Cycle Costs are explained in some detail in the following discussion.

LIFE CYCLE COST FACTORS

Life cycle costs include system development, purchase, installation, integration test, operation, maintenance, and upgrade through the expected life of the system. These costs generally fall into two main categories: (1) initial nonrecurring costs and (2) recurring costs. These categories, discussed in the following paragraphs, are tabulated in Appendix A.

Nonrecurring Costs

The major initial costs are for hardware, software, and systems integration. It is assumed that the entire system would be procured under a single contract and therefore, except where specified, the costs are not broken down into the specific categories.

The expenses of procurement and site installation/modification are in addition to the actual costs of the hardware. Procurement costs include the development of detailed specifications, preparation of a request for proposal, hardware acceptance, and contract negotiations. Procurement costs were not included in this analysis because it was assumed that they would be the same for all alternatives. Depending on the alternative, site installation/modification costs are included in the purchase price and, where applicable, are broken down.

Software costs will vary depending upon the hardware proposed. Costs of the software itself include the actual purchase cost of off-the-shelf items such as the operating system plus modifications, development of new software, test and integration, and documentation. Unless otherwise broken down, software costs are included in the purchase price.

Recurring Costs

In addition to operations, the major recurring costs are for hardware and software maintenance. Maintenance costs include maintenance contract costs, or in-house personnel where applicable, and implementation of new hardware/software updates.

Financial Costs

Inflation, discount rates, and the actual residual value of the system at the end of the life cycle are normally considered in determining life cycle cost factors. Financial costs will not impact the recommendation; therefore, we have not used inflation and discount rates in this study.

COST ANALYSIS

This section provides an analysis of the life cycle costs of the alternative candidates described in Chapter 5. The life cycle is assumed to be one year for development and seven years for system operation.

Unless otherwise specified, the costs of systems engineering, integration, test and verification, documentation, coordination of changes, training, and the other functions of systems engineering and integration are assumed to be included in the hardware costs. Figure 6-2 delineates the general assumptions used for the cost

Cost Analysis

Hardware costs	Market value
Software costs	Market value
Life cycle	1-year development*
	7-year operation

Network site costs for equipment and office per month, $1000. This would include an office for a network administrator plus miscellaneous office and monitor equipment supplies.

Initial 2500-data-device capability with growth per year of 500 devices for five years, expanding to a 5000-data-device capability (i.e., two devices per office).

Digital PBX will be initially wired for 1000 voice-only and 5000 voice and data devices.

Hardware and software maintenance will be on a contractual basis.

System engineering and integration costs are included in the purchase price.

The geographical scope includes all of the main building, approximately 360 offices in Building B (potential growth to 600 offices), and approximately 75 offices in Building A.
*PBX requires a two-year development period and includes complete rewiring.

Figure 6-2 General Assumptions

analysis. Assumptions that are alternative specific are discussed in their respective subsections.

Hardware costs are based on current prices. No attempt was made to select the lowest priced vendor, nor were quantity purchase discounts taken into consideration. LANs are an emerging technology; therefore, costs currently are relatively high, but can be expected to become lower as the technology develops. An assumption is made that hardware maintenance will be on a contractual basis.

Initial software costs are assumed to be included with the initial network purchase unless otherwise specified. Costs for custom-developed software are not included in the analysis. An assumption is made that software maintenance will be on a contractual basis.

Personnel costs are based on the assumption of one person for the position of network administrator. The cost for the position of network administrator, including overhead, was established at $100,000 per year.

Site costs for the network administrator's office plus miscellaneous office and monitoring equipment supplies were established at $1000 per month.

PBX LAN Cost Analysis

The PBX LAN cost analysis is based on Company X's system. The system is designed as a nonblocking, digital communications switch with the capability of digital voice and data integration. The network is based on a star topology, which is distributed into 32 modules of 256 ports each, for a total capacity of 8192 ports.

The cost analysis for the PBX LAN is based on an initial configuration of 3500 voice-only and 2500 voice/data lines. The final configuration includes 1000 voice-only and 5000 voice/data instruments. Figure 6-3 lists the hardware costs for the digital PBX alternative, while Figure 6-4 illustrates the projected life cycle costs. A specific hardware cost breakdown is not included because the PBX vendors will not provide this information.

Equipment	Description	Quantity	Price in $K
Master control unit (MCU)	The MCU provides the overall control of the system call processing and supervisory functions and contains the following units: two 32-bit processors, two 67 Mbyte disks, a 1600 BPI magnetic tape unit, a communication switch, and a 200 character per second line printer	2	
Switching network	Performs the switching function for each interface multiplexer	2	
Interface multiplexer	Provides the system interface to the telephone instruments	24	
System consoles	Perform program loading, system start-up/shutdown, diagnostics, disk formatting, and software modifications	2	
Integrated terminal equipment	Provides voice and data capability to user	5000	
Standard telephone equipment	Provides voice capability to user	1000	
Total			$6890

Note: Cost of twisted pair cable is included in the installation cost.

Figure 6-3 PBX LAN Hardware Costs

Baseband LAN Cost Analysis

The baseband cost analysis is based on the Company Y Local Area Network, which is based on the Cambridge-Ring Technology and uses token passing to support up to 500 data terminal equipment units (DTE) within a 15-mile circumference. A twin RG-59 coaxial cable forms the ring and provides DTE access through plug-in connectors. Equipment connection can be made anywhere along the ring, as required by the users. A conceptual configuration using this alternative would require 10 interconnected baseband rings to provide connectivity for 5000 user devices. Figure 6-5

	DEV Yr 1	DEV Yr 2[3]	OPR Yr 1	OPR Yr 2	OPR Yr 3	OPR Yr 4	OPR Yr 5	OPR Yr 6	OPR Yr 7	Total
HARDWARE										
Cost	2820	2820	250	250	250	250	250	—	—	6890
Installation[1]	750	750	—	—	—	—	—	—	—	1500
Maintenance	—	—	276	276	276	276	276	276	276	1932
SOFTWARE										
Cost[2]	—	—	—	—	—	—	—	—	—	
Maintenance[2]	—	—	—	—	—	—	—	—	—	
Personnel Operations	100	100	100	100	100	100	100	100	100	900
Site Facilities	12	12	12	12	12	12	12	12	12	108
Total	3682	3682	638	638	638	638	638	388	388	11330

Note:
[1] Includes new inside and outside cable plant wiring.
[2] Included with hardware costs.
[3] PBX LAN requires two-year development phase.

Figure 6-4 PBX Lan Projected Costs (In Thousands of Dollars)

Equipment	Description	Quantity	Price in $K
Twin coaxial cable	RG-59 teflon	32,000 ft	28
Network director	Network controller	20	182
Cable access point (CAP)	Provides interface between cable and TAP	2520	302
Terminal access point (TAP)	Provides interface between CAP and DTE	2500	4987
Total			5499

Figure 6-5 Baseband LAN Hardware Costs

delineates the hardware costs for this alternative, while Figure 6-6 illustrates the projected life cycle costs.

Broadband LAN Cost Analysis

The broadband cost analysis is based on the Company Z broadband LAN. This configuration consists of a CATV coaxial cable plant, headend frequency converter, and RF modem equipped with network interface units. The CATV cable plant is based on a mid-split design with a present capacity of five 6-MHz TV channels. The channels operate at a rate of 5 megabits per second. Connection to the cable is provided through a standard CATV tap. The cost analysis is based on an eventual five-channel network with a minimum capacity of 5000 data devices. Figure 6-7 delineates hardware costs, while Figure 6-8 illustrates the projected life cycle costs for this alternative.

Hybrid LAN Cost Analysis

The hybrid LAN cost analysis is based on a baseband/broadband configuration. The broadband network would be installed in the main building; the adjacent buildings would be internetted by a baseband system. Company Y has both a baseband and a broadband system; it was chosen for the cost analysis because of the existing compatability between the networks. Figure 6-9 lists the hardware costs, and Figure 6-10 illustrates the projected life cycle costs for the hybrid LAN.

Results

Figure 6-11 is a comparison of the results of the cost analysis for each alternative. In each case, the configuration was sized to support the initial capacity of 2500 data devices, with a proportional growth to 5000 data devices at the end of the fifth operating year. No discounts were assumed, so that any specifically available discounts at procurement time (expected to be 10 to 25 percent of hardware costs) are an additional source of cost reduction. Thus, the cost analysis represents a long-term and generally pessimistic view of life cycle costs.

	DEV Yr 1	OPR Yr 1	OPR Yr 2	OPR Yr 3	OPR Yr 4	OPR Yr 5	OPR Yr 6	OPR Yr 7	Total
HARDWARE									
Cost	2764	547	547	547	547	547	—	—	5499
Installation[1]	253	5	5	5	5	5	—	—	278
Maintenance[2]	—	151	178	206	234	273	289	289	1620
SOFTWARE[3]									
Cost									
Maintenance									
Personnel Operations	100	100	100	100	100	100	100	100	800
Site Facilities	12	12	12	12	12	12	12	12	96
Total	3129	815	842	870	878	937	401	401	8293

Note: [1] Includes engineering estimate of $100K for cabling between buildings.
[2] Maintenance costs based upon 5% of total cost per year.
[3] Included with hardware costs.

Figure 6-6 Baseband LAN Projected Costs (In Thousands of Dollars)

Equipment	Description	Quantity	Price in $K
Coaxial cable	RG-6 teflon	32,000 ft.	48
Network configuration facility (NCF)	Network controller provides network configuration	2	17.3
Application processor board	Provides interface for NCF	2	4
Single channel translator	Translates reverse frequencies for forward transmissions	5	17.5
Translator switchover unit	Provides switchover capability to redundant NCF		1
Network interface unit (NIU)	Provides interfaces for 6 data devices	836	7682
Total			7770

Figure 6-7 Broadband LAN Hardware Costs

TRADE-OFF ANALYSIS

The four alternatives were given a rating using the weighted matrix methodology described at the beginning of this chapter. The highest alternative was given a rating of one. The other alternatives were given a representative rating based on the ratio of their rating to the highest alternative. Each of the other criteria was then rated using the same methodology. As explained previously, the method is subjective, as a specific mathematical relationship could not be shown in each case.

After the ratings were assigned, the weighted ratings were developed by multiplying the weights by the ratings for each criterion. To determine the combined value, the weighted ratings were totalled for each alternative. The following is an analysis of each criterion for all alternatives.

System Availability and Reliability

The transmission media for all four alternatives are extremely reliable. Component failures are more likely to be due to physical damage caused by accidents than to structural imperfections. A poor installation could result in connector and other problems with any of the alternatives.

The hardware required for connecting a host to the LAN would have approximately the same level of reliability. A failure would only reduce the availability of a single host for any alternative.

In regard to switching, monitoring, and control equipment, there is a considerable difference between the digital PBX and the other alternatives. The digital PBX

	DEV YR 1	OPR YR 1	OPR YR 2	OPR YR 3	OPR YR 4	OPR YR 5	OPR YR 6	OPR YR 7	Total
HARDWARE									
Cost	3929	769	768	768	768	768	–	–	7770
Installation[1]	510	–	–	–	–	–	–	–	510
Maintenance[2]	–	222	260	299	338	376	415	415	2320
SOFTWARE									
Cost[3]	7.5	5[4]	5[4]	5[4]	–	–	–	–	28
Maintenance	–	–	–	–	–	–	–	–	
Personnel Operations	100	100	100	100	100	100	100	100	800
Site Facilities	12	12	12	12	12	12	12	12	96
Total	4559	1108	1145	1184	1218	1256	527	527	11524

Note: [1]Includes engineering estimate of $100K for cabling between buildings, $100K for cable plant design, and all components except cable and 25% contingency.
[2]Maintenance costs based on 5% of total cost per year.
[3]Initial software price includes maintenance and updates.
[4]Additional software for channel bridges.

Figure 6-8 Broadband LAN Projected Costs (In Thousands of Dollars)

Equipment	Description	Quantity	Price in $K
Coaxial cable	RG-11 teflon RG-59	18,000 ft. 14,000 ft.	48
Network controller	Provides network configuration and control (2 for baseband and 2 for broadband)	4	34.6
Application processor board	Provides interface for network controller	4	8
Single channel translator	Translates reverse frequencies for forward transmissions	3	3.6
Translator switchover unit	Provides switchover capability to redundant translator	2	2
Network interface unit	Provides interfaces for data devices	838	6992
Total			7088

Figure 6-9 Hybrid LAN Hardware Costs

is subject to a single-point failure shutdown of the entire system if this failure occurs in the main switching unit. Additionally, a failure in any of the MUX units would result in all systems in that area being down. This single-point failure problem is somewhat alleviated, but not eliminated, by duplicating all of this equipment and having automatic-switchover hardware and software. This single-point failure potential exists due to the star topology of a PBX system and not due to the reliability of certain or combined units. Refer to Appendix B for more details on equipment redundancy and reliability.

Monitoring and control equipment in the other alternatives would not put a system down. Baseband requires a full-time director for each ring and broadband requires a full-time frequency translator unit; however, both of these are considerably less sophisticated than a digital PBX main switching unit and therefore are much less susceptible to failure and less costly to provide back-up and automatic transfer. Reference the physical layout diagrams discussed in Chapter 5, Candidate Alternatives, and the hardware as delineated under Life Cycle Cost Factors for verification of this analysis.

The broadband and hybrid alternatives would require only minimal redundant equipment, and neither system would be entirely down for a single-point failure with or without redundant equipment. The baseband system would have the highest rating of 1. At maximum, only one tenth of the network would be down if both a director unit and backup failed. Broadband and hybrid would receive ratings of 0.90. The

	DEV YR 1	OPR YR 1	OPR YR 2	OPR YR 3	OPR YR 4	OPR YR 5	OPR YR 6	OPR YR 7	Total
HARDWARE									
Cost	3592 [1]	700	699	699	699	699	—	—	7088
Installation	353	—	—	—	—	—	—	—	353
Maintenance [3]	—	197	232	267	302	337	372	372	2080
SOFTWARE									
Cost	13 [2]	5 [4]	4 [4]	5 [4]	—	—	—	—	28
Maintenance									
Personnel Operations	100	100	100	100	100	100	100	100	800
Site Facilities	12	12	12	12	12	12	12	12	96
Total	4070	1015	1048	1083	1113	1148	484	484	10445

Figure 6-10 Hybrid LAN Projected Costs (In Thousands of Dollars)

(1) Includes engineering estimate of $100K for cabling between buildings, 100K for cable plant design and all components except cable and 25% contingency.
(2) Initial cost includes maintenance and updates.
(3) Maintenance cost based on 5% of total cost per year.
(4) Additional software for channel bridges.

67

	PBX	Baseband	Broadband	Hybrid
HARDWARE				
Cost	6890	5499	7770	7088
Installation	1500	278	510	353
Maintenance	1932	1620	2320	2080
SOFTWARE				
Maintenance Cost	—	—	27.5	28
Personnel Operations	900	800	800	800
Site Facilities	108	96	96	96
TOTAL	11330	8293	11524	10445

Figure 6-11 Cost Comparison (In Thousands of Dollars)

digital PBX would receive the lowest rating because, although significant redundant equipment is provided to alleviate the single-point failure problems, considerably more hardware is required to be operational than is the case with baseband or broadband. Also, due to the intrinsic nature of star topology, the PBX is still susceptible to an entire system failure should the entire main switch unit become inoperable.

An additional problem with the digital PBX alternative concerns the reduced reliability at high data rates. Most PBX vendors that publish error rates guarantee only a 10^{-7} bit error rate (BER) for all frequencies. This is considerably lower than the computer industry requirement of 10^{-9} BER for magnetic tape unit and disk drive data transfers. BER for broadband and baseband systems range from 10^{-9} to 10^{-13} as cited in *Datapro Reports on Data Communications* 1983.

Studies by American Telephone and Telegraph Company (AT&T) concerning error rates of standard telephone lines (twisted-pair) indicate an alarmingly high error rate with the high-speed use of telephone circuits. James Martin's book, *Telecommunications and the Computer* (1976, Prentice-Hall, pp. 558-560), summarizes these studies and indicates that "error rate tends to increase rapidly as transmission speeds are raised above 4800 bps, and at such speeds is so variable that reliable statistics are not published." These studies were applied to voice-grade circuits and are not entirely applicable to digital PBXs. However, the problem AT&T had with twisted pair is directly applicable, as digital PBX installations use this identical wiring. This study deliberately avoided certain panel and step-by-step central offices that were subject to transient electronic disturbances or "noise." Refer to Appendix C, Error Rate Supplement, for more information on this topic.

All LAN vendors predict optimistic up-time versus down-time for their systems. Actual figures could not be obtained because of relatively new installations; therefore, no comparison was made between baseband, broadband, and digital PBX.

Because of the possibility of single-point failures, although extremely low because of redundancy, and the excessive bit error rate, the digital PBX was given a rating of 0.6 for System Availability and Reliability.

Response Time

The digital PBX, using star topology, essentially presents only the delay time associated with the MUX for any transmission; therefore, this system would receive the highest rating, 1. The other alternatives use communication protocols (CSMA/CD or token ring) which can cause delays, depending upon the type and frequency of data transmitted. These delays can either be random or deterministic, depending upon the specific type of protocol. All alternatives were designed with the objective of meeting system requirements with the projected throughput traffic; however, with increases in the loading factor, the broadband approach is favored. The baseband approach utilizes a single channel and access is not based on contention. Increases in the loading factor increase response time. With the broadband approach, multiple channels are available. As response time becomes a problem with broadband, a new channel can be added. When the total number of channels available in one band is full, another band can be implemented. Broadband was given a slightly higher rating, 0.95, than baseband, 0.90.

Growth Capability

The major limiting factor in determining the growth capability and flexibility for the alternative designs is system bandwidth. Digital PBX has an actual bandwidth of 1.5 MHz due to twisted pair frequency limitation. In certain circumstances, 10 MHz can be transmitted if the data is of a bursty nature. This is accomplished by a store and transmit procedure. Baseband has a bandwidth of 10 MHz and broadband, 450 MHz. Both digital PBX and baseband will support limited high-speed data transfers and video applications, while broadband virtually has no limit regarding high-speed data transfers, conferencing, or full-frequency video simultaneously transmitted with other data and voice. The general tendency in computer processing is toward higher speed devices, such as high-speed graphics and laser printing. Broadband can expand to multiple channels, while baseband has a single channel limitation. Digital PBX using baseband connectivity has this same limitation.

Broadband has the highest rating, 1.0, regarding growth capability, with baseband and digital PBX having lower ratings of 0.6 and 0.5 respectively.

Training Requirements and Ease of Operation

Training requirements and ease of operation were rated equal for all approaches. The network should be transparent to the users. Training should only be of concern for the desirable features of a network, such as monitoring and special control.

Compatibility and Connectivity

Nearly all vendors of each alternative claim compatibility with common conductor and protocol standards. This should be rated equal for each alternative, as the network, when installed, would then become the standard.

Connectivity is quite different for the digital PBX than for baseband or broadband. Implementation of the broadband alternative requires the installation of a single coaxial cable with the appropriate number of drops. The baseband alternative requires a dual cable with the appropriate number of drops. The baseband cable could be less rigid and more easily installed than broadband. Digital PBX, however, requires the installation of two twisted pairs from each device to each multiplex unit. This would mean 500 twisted pairs for each of the 24 multiplexers to prewire 6000 units. Physically, 100 pairs of 24 AWG wire represent a cable one inch in diameter. This creates a significant installation problem in regard to the constraints on architectural changes to the physical structure. All vendors contacted recommended installation of new wiring. Also, the placement of multiplexers would not coincide with existing telephone-terminal–central-wiring locations.

Rating for broadband and baseband would be equal, 1.0, as a trade-off exists concerning the dual, easier-to-install cable of baseband and the single, more-difficult-to-install broadband cable. Broadband cable is larger and more rigid. As hybrid is a combination of broadband and baseband it would receive a rating of 1.0, also. Digital PBX would receive a rating of 0.8.

Maintenance and Logistics Support

The baseband system has been in operation longer, is a well-proven system, and will definitely have fewer maintenance problems on a component basis. In addition, the baseband system has less hardware than the digital PBX. Because of the 10 networks for baseband versus the five channels for the broadband (see Chapter 5 for system descriptions), the difference in hardware quantity between the two is negligible. Maintenance of the hybrid alternative design would include both broadband and baseband technology and be more difficult because of the additional different types of hardware.

The digital PBX would achieve the lowest rating, due to the greater amount and type of equipment required. The digital PBX is a relatively new design with regard to high-speed data. Due to the inherent nature of a system not yet fully utilized, unknown problems may surface. Baseband technology for digital communication was in use years prior to digital PBX or broadband. Equipment used in the broadband system has been used extensively in cable TV in harsh environments with a relatively low number of component failures. Refer to the hardware charts in Figures 6-3, 6-5, 6-7, and 6-9, for delineation of the types of hardware for each alternative.

Baseband has been assigned the highest rating, and digital PBX the lowest.

Security

There are two forms of security involved with a typical LAN. The primary means of security concerns the physical security of the individual systems and their protection through software control. Since the use of encryption devices is not a requirement and sensitive data are only software-protected, the use of physical security measures becomes an important consideration. Most existing government computer installations are required to have security analyses performed on their data processing systems. For this reason, the various alternatives were rated according to their ability to provide physical security protection.

Broadband and baseband coaxial cable must be physically tapped. Digital-PBX-twisted-pair cabling, however, would not require a physical connection for the monitoring of any data transmitted on the cable. Information transmitted on twisted pair wire can be inductively acquired by placing sensitive pick-up devices near the wire, with no electronic evidence that the information has been accepted. This would make detection of illegal acquisition of data nearly impossible. Broadband and baseband alternatives both received the highest rating, with the digital PBX design being assigned a 0.9.

Transition Impact

In our example, new LAN equipment would be installed and checked out, followed by the cabling for the LAN and the connection and checkout of each of the hosts, on a system-by-system basis. With the exception of the digital PBX, these phases would essentially be the same. As identified previously, the digital PBX requires the installation and check-out of 500 twisted pair cable for each of the 24 multiplexers. Due to the problem of capacitive and inductive pickup on unshielded twisted pair cable, extra care must be given to placement of these 24,000 wires. Digital PBX vendors recommend not using existing phone lines and predict a two-year installation versus less than one year for other alternative LANs. All alternatives other than PBX receive the highest rating; digital PBX receives a 0.9.

Relative Life Cycle Costs

This rating is not subjective. The lowest-cost alternative receives the highest rating and the others are proportionally assigned by a mathematical process. Baseband has the lowest life cycle costs and receives a rating of 1.

WEIGHTED RATING COMPARISON

The weighted rating comparison in Figure 6-12 has been completed for all alternatives. In the trade-off analysis only the digital PBX, baseband, and broadband were discussed; the hybrid alternative was interpreted from the broadband and baseband ratings.

Results of the analysis and weighted ratings indicate that the broadband has the highest total weighted ratings.

CRITERIA	WEIGHT	PBX Rating	PBX Weighted rating	BASEBAND Rating	BASEBAND Weighted rating	BROADBAND Rating	BROADBAND Weighted rating	HYBRID Rating	HYBRID Weighted rating
SYSTEM AVAILABILITY AND RELIABILITY	20	0.60	12.0	1.00	20.0	0.95	19.0	0.95	19.0
RESPONSE TIME	5	1.00	5.0	0.90	4.5	0.95	4.8	0.90	4.5
GROWTH CAPABILITY	15	0.50	7.5	0.60	9.0	1.00	15.0	0.90	13.5
TRAINING	5	1.00	5.0	1.00	5.0	1.00	5.0	1.00	5.0
COMPATIBILITY AND CONNECTIVITY	10	0.80	8.0	1.00	10.0	1.00	10.0	1.00	10.0
MAINTENANCE	10	0.90	9.0	1.00	10.0	0.98	9.8	0.90	9.0
SECURITY	5	0.90	4.5	1.00	5.0	1.00	5.0	1.00	5.0
TRANSITION	15	0.90	13.5	1.00	15.0	1.00	15.0	1.00	15.0
LIFE CYCLE COSTS	15	0.73	11.0	1.00	15.0	0.72	10.8	0.79	11.9
TOTALS	100		75.5		93.5		94.4		92.9

Figure 6-12 Weighted Ratings Chart

7

Conceptual Design

This chapter will present a conceptual design of the broadband LAN selected in our example. The LAN configuration will be explained with reference to the model described in Chapter 3.

The elements of this model will be discussed individually in terms of operating parameters and quantities of elements required to meet the requirements of the LAN. There is no single solution to the synthesis of a network to support multiple users with many different services. Therefore, many possible solutions may be tested through the use of the model for the message network by performing the calculations with different input parameters. As the network requirements become better defined, the variability of the inputs to the process will decrease; however, there will still be enough flexibility to allow multiple solutions in most cases.

In this chapter one acceptable solution will be derived through the use of the model, but it is not to be construed as the only possible solution. There was no intention to favor any specific vendor; therefore, the parameters used in the demonstrated solution will not intentionally be vendor oriented. To derive a solution for a particular vendor's products, it will be necessary to repeat the process with input parameters based upon those product specifications.

PHYSICAL NETWORK

The network is assumed to be a broadband network with a radio frequency subsystem as the transmission medium. The radio-frequency subsystem includes the cable and all passive and active RF components. The components and their electrical characteristics are shown in Figure 7-1. These characteristics match those of the special

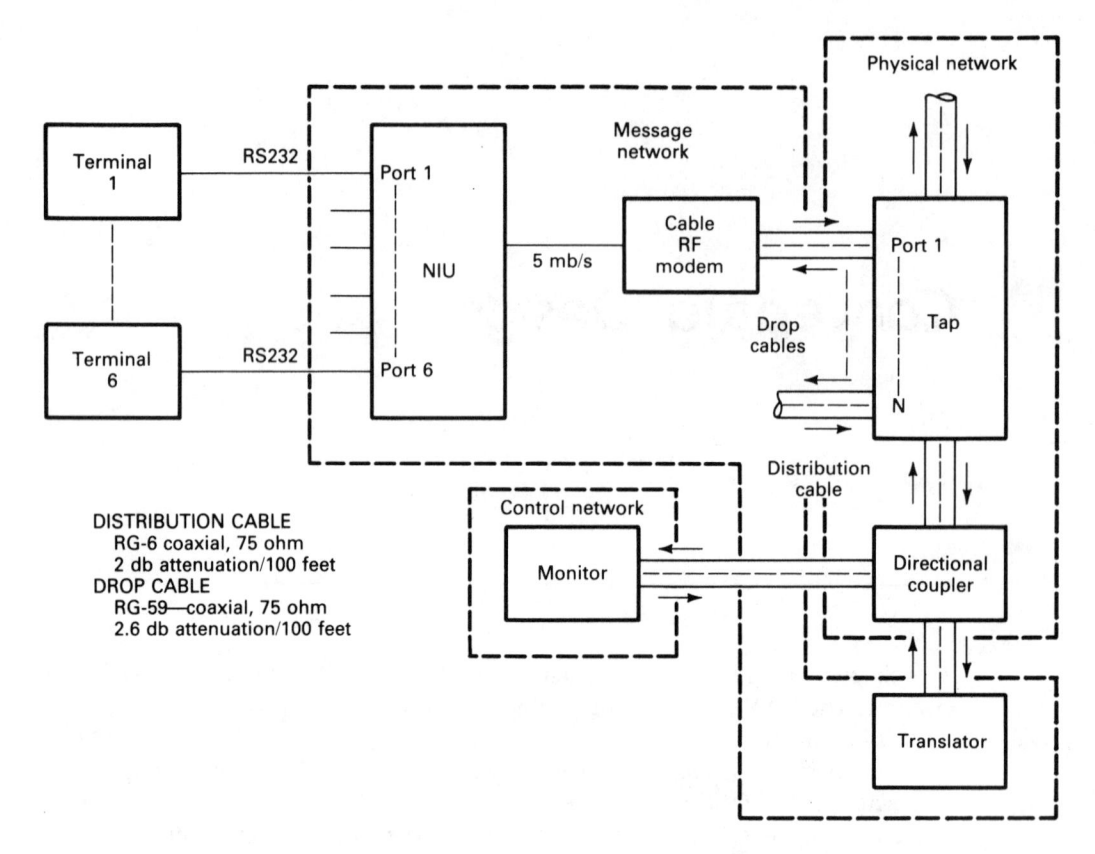

Figure 7-1 Packetized Data Interface

cable that is commonly used in the cable TV industry. Passive components include directional couplers, splitters, and taps. The characteristics of commonly available examples are given in Figure 7-2.

The distribution of passive components in a cable plant for a typical single floor of our example facility is given in the layout of Figure 7-3, while a detailed breakdown of the components as used in the layout is given in Figure 7-4. The detailed network design consists of selection of components which exhibit characteristics that allow end-to-end signal levels that are within the operational values of the active RF components. The results of this process as applied to the extreme ends of circuits A and C from the layout in Figure 7-3 are shown in Figure 7-5 and Figure 7-6.

The taps are available in several configurations, and each configuration may be selected from a wide range of attenuation values that are available. The active components consist of the RF modems, frequency translators, and amplifiers. The RF modem is the point of origination of the RF carrier signal in a 6 MHz-wide channel between 5.75 and 60 MHz. This reverse channel signal is transmitted at a nominal level of 35 dBmV, but arrives at the headend at an attenuated level of near −10

Physical Network 75

DAX 746 (RF DATA EXCHANGE UNIT)	Transmit Level 35 dBmV	+5 dB −15 dB
	Receive Level 10 dBmV ± 10 dB	
DAX 1009 TRANSLATOR	Freq. Shift - 156.25 MHz	
	Gain - 45 dB ±5 dB	
	Maximum Output - 50 dBmV Level	

Splitters and Directional Couplers	Attenuation dB Below Input		
	1	2	3
STC−3D	3.9	3.9	N/A
STC−8D	1.7	9.0	N/A
STC−12D	1.3	13.0	N/A
STC−3−636D	4.1	7.4	7.4

TAPS	Number of Ports	Attenuation Range in dB
FFT−8	8	10.5 - 41.2 Selectable
FFT−4	4	6.8 - 41.5 Selectable
FFT−2	2	3.2 - 41.0 Selectable

Figure 7-2 Equipment Characteristics

dBmV. At the translator, a conversion of plus 156.25 MHz takes place and the signal is amplified by approximately 45 dB. The 35 dBmV level signal in the forward channel then traverses the passive network path to the intended receiver, where it arrives at a level of approximately − 10 dBmV.

The active components are adjustable within a limited range; therefore, the installation process includes tuning the network and verification by test that the pre-

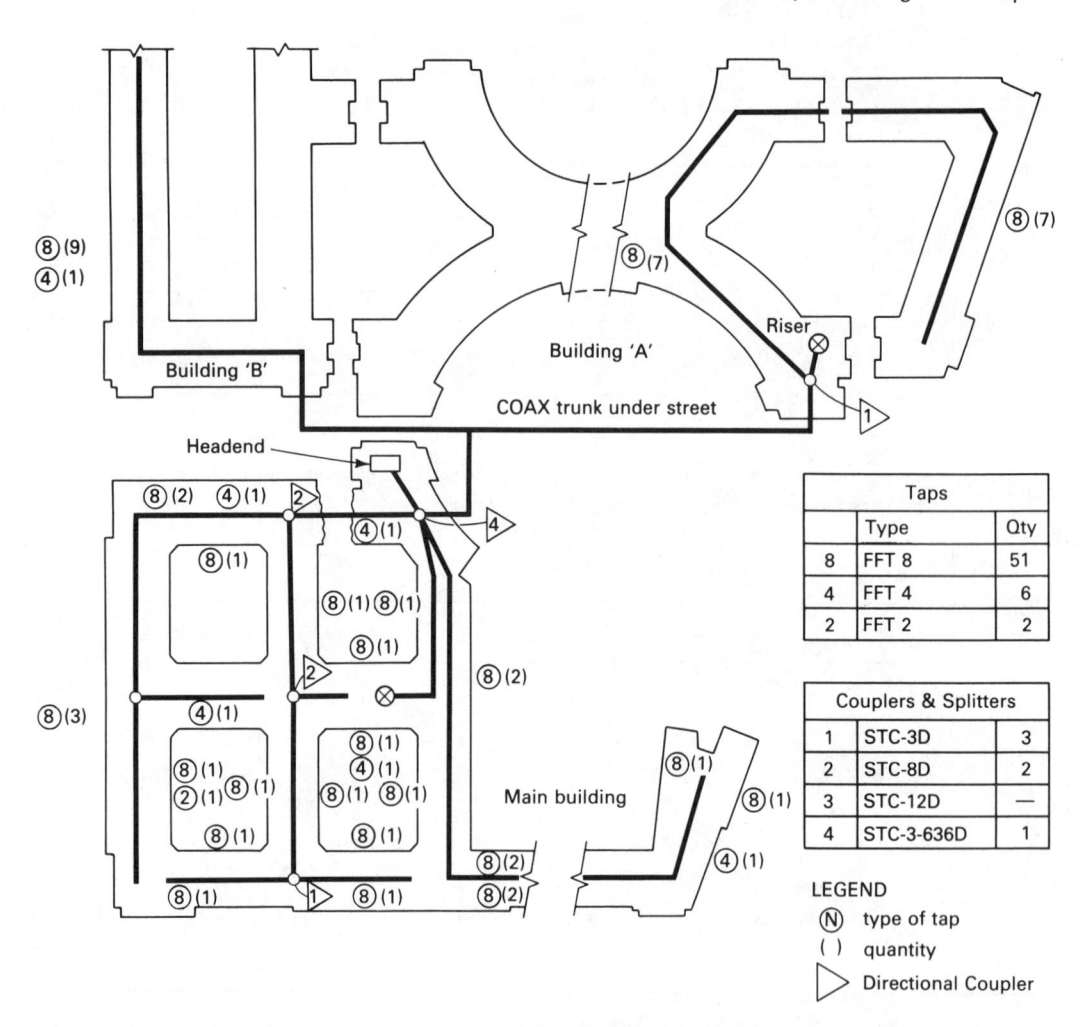

Figure 7-3 Broadband Typical Circuit Layout

dicted numbers are met. Some adjustable components must serve multiple paths, so adjustment of these components must be followed by signal strength testing of all affected nodes.

MESSAGE NETWORK

The message network consists of the combination of hardware and software necessary to implement the user services. The process needed to synthesize this part of the LAN involves the calculation of the number of messages represented by the peak throughput rate required for the network.

Message Network   77

CIRCUIT DESCRIPTION (REF FLOOR 6)

ITEM \ CIRCUIT	A	B	C	D	E	F	TOTAL
OFFICES	78	87	86	55	55	75	436
NIUs							TBD
RF MODEMS							TBD
TAPS							
FFT-8	10	10	8	7	7	9	51
FFT-4	1	2	2				5
FFT-2			2				2
STC-3D		1	1	1			3
STC-8D		2					2
STC-12D							-
STC-3-636D	1	1					2
CABLE LENGTH	682'	506'	586'	900'	900'	750'	
/LOSS in dB	8.2	6.1	7.0	10.8	10.8	9.0	

HEADEND DESCRIPTION

Model	Description	Qty
TBD	Translator 6 MHz B/W	5
TBD	Power suppy	5

Figure 7-4 Broadband Circuit Description (Typical)

Requirements and Assumptions

The peak throughput rate is based upon the requirement surveys documented in Chapter 4, or 173 Kbps. A growth factor of 10 has been applied to derive the peak throughput of 1.73 Mbps. In order to develop a model for further calculation of network parameters, several assumptions were made. The potential for problems inherent in the use of specifications that favor a specific manufacturer was avoided by the use of IEEE 802 committee values. If the specifics of IEEE 802 are not known, then Ethernet values are used, since this product is considered to be the de facto standard for cable-based LANs. The list of assumptions used is given in Figure 7-7. The packet length of 512 bits is the minimum length of an Ethernet packet. The use of this packet length represents the most severe case in terms of contention for the network, because the largest number of users would be contending for a given network time period.

	Gain/Loss (dB)	Level (dBmV)
TRANSMIT LEVEL	ADJUSTED	36.4
Tap	− 10.5	25.9
Cable	− 8.2	17.7
Dual splitter	− 4.1	13.6
Dual splitter	− 4.1	9.5
Taps (7)	− 18.2	− 8.7*
Translator	+ 45	36.3
Taps (7)	− 20.3	16
Cable	− 8.2	7.8
Dual splitter	− 4.1	3.7
Dual splitter	− 4.1	− 0.4
Tap	− 10.5	− 10.9
RECEIVE LEVEL		− 10.9

*at Headend

Figure 7-5 Circuit A, End-to-End Circuit Losses

	Gain/Loss (dB)	Level (dBmV)
TRANSMIT LEVEL	ADJUSTED	39.0
Tap	− 3.2	35.8
Dual Splitter	− 7.4	28.4
Direct coupler	− 1.7	26.7
Splitter	− 3.9	22.8
Taps - 8 (7)	− 18.2	4.6
Taps - 4	− 6.8	− 2.2
Taps - 2	− 3.2	− 5.4*
Translator	+ 45	39.6
Tap	− 3.2	36.4
Dual splitter	− 7.4	29.0
Direct coupler	− 1.7	27.3
Splitter	− 3.9	23.4
Taps - 8 (7)	− 18.2	5.2
Taps - 4	− 6.8	− 1.6
Taps - 2	− 3.2	− 4.8
RECEIVE LEVEL		− 4.8

*at Headend

Figure 7-6 Circuit C, End-to-End Circuit Losses

Message Network

1. Topology - Coaxial cable bus
2. Data rate (on the bus) - 10Mbps (Ethernet)
3. Packet length - 512 bits (Ethernet)
   a. Information field - 368 bits
   b. Header - 144 bits
4. Cable dialectric - polyethyline foam (propagation time = .79 c where c = velocity of light)
5. Cable length - 1 kilometer
6. Slot time - 512 bit periods (Ethernet)
7. Access method - CSMA/CD

Figure 7-7 Network Model Assumptions

With the given peak data rate of 1.73 Mbps, there would be 4701 messages per second on the network at 512 bits per message. With a message length of 4000 bytes (4000 × 8 bits/byte = 32,000 bits) there would be 54 messages per second. As shown in Figure 7-8, the maximum capacity of a 10 Mbps channel is 7.19 Mbps; therefore, the 1.73 Mbps peak data throughput rate constitutes approximately 25 percent of the absolute maximum possible throughput in a noncontention application. The use of contention reduces the mean maximum throughput by an indeterminate amount since the delays encountered will be randomly generated. However, through the use

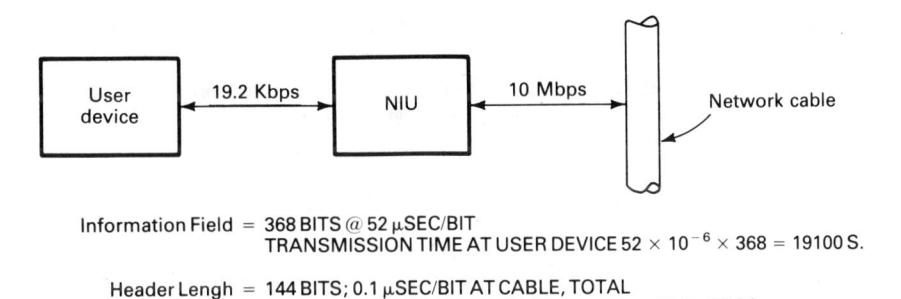

Information Field = 368 BITS @ 52 μSEC/BIT
TRANSMISSION TIME AT USER DEVICE 52 × 10^{-6} × 368 = 19100 S.

Header Lengh = 144 BITS; 0.1 μSEC/BIT AT CABLE, TOTAL
MESSAGE LENGTH 512 BITS. (T message = 51.2 μSEC.)

T message = 368 + 144 bits = 512 bits

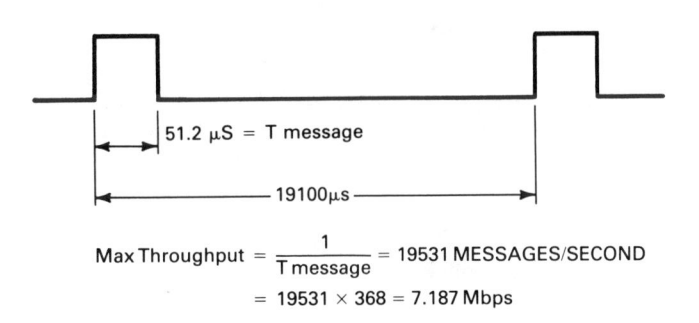

51.2 μS = T message
19100 μs

$$\text{Max Throughput} = \frac{1}{T \text{ message}} = 19531 \text{ MESSAGES/SECOND}$$
$$= 19531 \times 368 = 7.187 \text{ Mbps}$$

Figure 7-8 User Device/Cable Interface

of a packet-interval ratio to provide a high probability of a nonjamming network, the maximum mean throughput reduction may be estimated.

The packet interval ratio is based upon a widely accepted assumption* of 2e collisions per successful transmission with contention accessing. The formula for deriving this message ratio (R) is as follows:

$$\text{Total Time} = \text{T Message} + 2e \,(\text{T Slot})$$

Where T Slot is defined as cable propagation time plus circuit delays.

$$R = \frac{\text{Total Time}}{\text{T Message}}$$

In this case,

$$R = \frac{51.2 + 5.436 \times 51.2}{51.2}$$

$$R = 6.34$$

The calculations in the following section use this factor in the determination of the number of channels required to support the required data traffic.

Channel/User Device Trade-Off Analysis

Using the requirements and assumptions defined in the previous section, the first step in designing the message network is to determine the minimum number of channels required, as well as the number of user devices utilizing each channel. The second step involves simulating peak throughput for each channel and determining the expected average delay. If the delay is not acceptable, then the process is repeated, using an increased number of channels. Once the number of channels and user devices per channel have been determined, the quantity of translators, NIUs, and bridges can be established.

A message ratio of 6.34:1 has been established as desirable to achieve a nonjamming network and yet maintain maximum throughput. With a packet size of 512 bits, the possible number of packets transmitted per second on a 10 Mbps channel, assuming the above message ratio, would be 3080 according to the following calculations:

$$\frac{10^7 \text{ bits/sec}}{(512 \text{ bits/packet} \times 6.34)} = 3080 \text{ packets/sec}$$

With a 512-bit packet there are 144 bits of overhead, leaving 368 bits of actual data (see Figure 7-7). Using 1.73 Mbps as the peak data-throughput rate, and 368 bits of data per packet, the LAN would be required to accommodate 4700 packets per second. The calculations follow:

$$\frac{1.73 \times 10^6 \text{ bits/sec}}{368 \text{ bits/packet}} = 4700 \text{ packets/sec}$$

*See Bart Struck, Bell Laboratories, "Which Local Net Bus Access is Most Sensitive to Traffic Congestion," *Data Communications*, January 1983.

Message Network

This can easily be handled with a two-channel system with a margin of over 30 percent per channel, as illustrated by the following ratio:

$$\frac{4700 \text{ packets/sec required}}{3080 \text{ packets/sec channel possible}} = 1.59 \text{ channels}$$

Dividing the 5000 potential user devices and the packet-per-second requirement equally between channels would result in 2500 user devices transmitting 2350 packets per second. In order to simulate the message delay, a worst-case situation has been established where all user devices attempt to transmit at the average rate of m = 2350/2500 or 0.94 message per second. A window for each packet, to allow for CMSA/CD, is established as 1534 bit spaces. This was determined by using three packet spaces and removing the end bits of the internal packet. These packet spaces were selected as a worst-case number allowing no transmission for a 511-bit time period prior to or after the transmission of the actual packets. At the 10 Mbps rate, there are 6500 windows, or spaces, for packets in each second.

Using the Poisson distribution as a model for the contention rate for the 6500 spaces, we can calculate the probability of multiple numbers of collisions during these spaces. The probability of x packets in a space is expressed as

$$P(x) = \frac{m^x e^{-m}}{x!}$$

The mathematical derivation of the maximum number of packets contending for a packet space and the number of retransmissions required to transmit all packets is provided in Appendix D. The scheduling of retransmissions is determined by a controlled randomization process resulting in a predictable delay (due to design) which is an integral multiple of the slot time of 51.2 microseconds. In this case, a maximum of four retransmissions are required, resulting in a designed delay of $2^n \times 51.2$ ms where n = 4 or 819 microseconds of delay. This is an acceptable delay and well within the LAN requirements, indicating that two channels, each with 2500 terminals, is a satisfactory design parameter for the LAN example.

Equipment Requirements

The message network consists of translators, NIUs, bridges, and gateways to interface the physical network to the user resources. The number of these units is based primarily upon the number of channels, user devices, and the interfaces to non-LAN sources and receptors of data; however, the choice of vendor will affect the ultimate design. Specifically, the packaging of multiple units within one chassis often results in a significant cost savings on the quantity units.

Since the trade-off analysis shows that two channels would be more than adequate for the LAN example, then a minimum of two frequency translators are required. These units, usually packaged in quantities of three, are the most important single piece of hardware in the LAN. The third unit is designated as a back-up for the prime translator and interfaces through an automatic switching unit.

There are between two and eight logical NIUs packaged in each physical unit.

The number of logical NIUs per unit is limited more by the physical distance between user devices than by any other criterion. Since the estimated number of user devices was based upon two per office, the physical requirements are not too much of a limitation. An estimate of six logical NIUs per unit should suffice in the case of separation of floors, buildings, and end locations. This would result in 834 physical units containing 5000 NIUs.

Since there are only two channels, only two bridges are required to interface one channel to the other. This equipment is not as essential as the translators; therefore, a back-up unit is not recommended.

CONTROL NETWORK

The control network consists of those devices that assist the network administrator in performing the functions necessary for the proper network maintenance, operation, and long-range planning of the LAN. These functions generally fall under two broad categories: monitoring and configuration control. The following subsections define a system that will provide the information needed by the network administrator.

Network Monitor

Real-time displays and historic printed reports are needed not only for performance measurement but for capacity planning as well. The information monitored and collected by the network monitor includes data on packet distribution, sources of delay, collision and retry counts, communication paths, throughput utilization, and equipment status. These statistics are useful in determining LAN traffic patterns and channel capacities as well as node and line status.

The commercially available network monitor that provides this monitoring capability is compatible with the physical and message network and is programmable. In addition to the monitoring of routine data on the network, the network monitor generates traffic on a periodic basis to test responses from the various nodes. This response is used to evaluate both host, nodal, and link status. An example of the display format is shown in Figures 7-9 through 7-12. Hard copies can be made of all displays on a local printer. All displays and printouts are operator-selectable and can be reformatted by the high-level program language provided with the monitor.

Data from the monitor can be accessed remotely from selected terminals on the LAN. The control functions described in the following subsection can also be acquired through the same terminal.

Failure of the monitor will not degrade operation of the LAN's physical or message network.

Network Controller

The standard NIU uses a numeric address to identify itself within the message network. Symbolic names are assigned to these addresses to facilitate operations by the

Control Network

PACKET DISTRIBUTION

Channel <u>2</u>　　　　Time Begin <u>1423</u>　　　　Period <u>60</u> Seconds

PACKET SIZE HISTOGRAM

Data Field Size	0 - 8	9 - 16	17 - 32	33 - 64
Number of Packets	<u>2120</u>	<u>610</u>	<u>810</u>	<u>521</u>
	65 - 128	129 - 256	257 - 512	513 - 1024
	<u>692</u>	<u>1324</u>	<u>1111</u>	<u>1281</u>

TRANSMISSION RECORD

Collision Counts <u>163</u>　　　　　　　　　　　　　　Retransmission Count <u>208</u>

Retry Time Interval Average <u>2.6</u> Milliseconds

Packet Arrival Interval Average <u>71</u> Milliseconds

Figure 7-9 Monitor/Controller Display, Packet Distribution

COMMUNICATION MATRICES

Time Begin <u>1423</u>　　　　Period <u>3600</u> Seconds

Source No. Begin <u>001001</u>　　　　End <u>001100</u>

Source	Destination	Packets
<u>001001</u>	001021	<u>1683</u>
	<u>001026</u>	<u>1522</u>
	<u>001136</u>	<u>681</u>
	<u>001142</u>	<u>2116</u>
<u>001002</u>	<u>002001</u>	<u>423</u>
<u>001021</u>	<u>001001</u>	<u>6</u>
<u>001026</u>	<u>001001</u>	<u>10</u>
<u>001136</u>	<u>001001</u>	<u>2</u>
<u>001142</u>	<u>001001</u>	<u>2</u>

Figure 7-10 Monitor/Controller Display, Communication Matrices

various users. The symbolic names, numeric addresses, topological configuration, and data rates are assigned and changed by the network administrator. Addresses and topographical configuration are changed as terminals are relocated. Data rates are altered based upon the rate of data to be transmitted or received. A directory of the names, addresses, topological configuration, and data rates is maintained by the network controller. A directory display is illustrated in Figure 7-13.

The network administrator controls user access to the network through the use of a password procedure in the network controller. The design of the controller should not prohibit the use of encryption devices.

CHANNEL THROUGHPUT

Channel No. 2	Time Begin 1423	Period 60	Seconds
Packets on Channel	24238	Terminals on Channel	101
Packets off Channel	142	Terminals off Channel	21
Total	24480	Total Characters	59433
CRC Errors	522	Data Characters	33230
No. of Collisions	241	Channel Utilization	44%
Average Delay, Milliseconds	1.1		

Figure 7-11 Monitor/Controller Display, Channel Throughput

LAN STATUS

Time Begin ___1423___   Period ___10___ Minutes
Test Transmission Count ___22___

Nodes Out	002163	002164	002191	003009
	004012	005001		
Branch Out				
Gateway Out				

Figure 7-12 Monitor/Controller Display, LAN Status

DIRECTORY

Sort by Symbolic (S) or Numeric (N) ___S___
Begin ___CMTS01___   End ___CMTS10___

NIU	Address	Data Rate
CMTS01	007001	19.2
CMTS02	007002	19.2
CMTS03	007003	19.2
CMTS04	007004	19.2
CMTS05	007005	19.2
CMTS06	008112	19.2
CMTS07	008122	19.2
CMTS08	008142	19.2
CMTS09	009063	19.2
CMTS10	009072	19.2

Change ? (Y/N) ___N___

Figure 7-13 Monitor/Controller Display, Directory

System Configuration

The controller and monitor are a single, integrated unit using a common terminal, printer, and operating system. Its connection to the physical network is through a single tap. The location is near the office of the network administrator.

CONCLUSION

This chapter utilized a network model to illustrate the technical approach used in developing the LAN conceptual design. The model can be used in the design of any LAN or the modification of an existing network. The mathematical formulas used in determining the optimum number of channels and the delay induced by the resultant number of user devices can be used to benchmark proposed systems for throughput and other parameters.

The LAN conceptual design developed within this chapter is not meant to be either the optimum or only solution. There are as many solutions as there are vendors, each with its advantages and disadvantages. This conceptual design intentionally did not advocate any specific manufacturer and will therefore enable a number of vendors to propose alternative designs that can be evaluated in an unbiased fashion.

Known and proposed LAN standards were used where possible. The model illustrates where these standards impose limitations on the design. As the standards become solidified, the final design could change. Of particular interest is a standard for the number of subchannels per channel. With more stringent throughput requirements, the addition of high volume user devices, and high volume systems, the use of dedicated subchannels could be advantageous. The full use of this model can still be employed even though the anticipated standards are yet to be developed.

Appendix A

Local Area Network Systems

Appendix A provides a representative sampling of profiles of local area network systems currently on the market. The systems are arranged by medium (twisted pair, baseband, and broadband). Each entry includes vendor information, technical specifications, standards supported, and additional explanatory notes where necessary. A more detailed listing can be found in *The Local Area Networking Directory* (third edition), published by Phillips Publishing, Inc. in 1983.

LAN CHARACTERISTICS

CORVUS SYSTEMS, INC.
NETWORK: OMNINET

TYPE	DATA TYPE	TOPOLOGY
Twisted Wire Pair	Digital	Bus

SPECIFICATIONS

Operating Mode(s): full duplex
Access Method(s): CSMA/CA
Transmission Medium(s): twisted pair
Data Transfer Rate(s): 1 Mbps
Number of Stations Supported: 64
Compatible Vendor Devices: Corvus, Apple, IBM, NEC, CED LS1-II
Maximum Distance Between Devices: 4000 feet
Communications Protocol(s) Supported: X.25 and SNA.
LAN Standards Supported
Proposed IEEE 802 Standard: no
ISO Open Systems Interconnection Reference Model (OSI): yes; hardware supports layers 1–4; software supports layers 5–7.

LAN CHARACTERISTICS

INTECOM, INC.
NETWORK: IBX S/40

TYPE	DATA TYPE	TOPOLOGY
Twisted Wire Pair	Digital, Audio	Star

SPECIFICATIONS

Operating Mode(s): full duplex
Access Method(s): CSMA/CD
Transmission Medium(s): fiber optics, twisted pair
Data Transfer Rate(s): 57.6 Kbps
Number of Stations Supported: 4096
Compatible Vendor Devices: any RS-232C or RS-449 device
Maximum Distance Between Devices: 29,000 feet
Communications Protocol(s) Supported: IBM 3270, X.25
<u>LAN Standards Supported</u>
Proposed IEEE 802 Standard: N/A
ISO Open Systems Interconnection Reference Model (OSI): N/A

LAN CHARACTERISTICS

DATA CONTROL SYSTEMS
NETWORK: CCM-200

TYPE	DATA TYPE	TOPOLOGY
Twisted Wire Pair	Digital	Bus

SPECIFICATIONS

Operating Mode(s): full duplex
Access Method(s): polling
Transmission Medium(s): coaxial cable
Data Transfer Rate(s): 19.2 kilobaud
Number of Stations Supported: 1000
Compatible Vendor Devices: any RS-232 device
Maximum Distance Between Devices: 10 miles
Communications Protocol(s) Supported: transparent to protocols
<u>LAN Standards Supported</u>
Proposed IEEE 802 Standard: no
ISO Open Systems Interconnection Reference Model (OSI): no

LAN CHARACTERISTICS

DATA GENERAL CORPORATION—INFORMATION SYSTEMS DIVISION (ISD)
NETWORK: XODIAC

TYPE	DATA TYPE	TOPOLOGY
Baseband	Digital	Bus

SPECIFICATIONS

Operating Mode(s): half duplex
Access Method(s): token passing
Transmission Medium(s): coaxial cable
Data Transfer Rate(s): 2 Mbps
Number of Stations Supported: 32 processors
Compatible Vendor Devices: IBM
Maximum Distance Between Devices: 1 mile
Communications Protocol(s) Supported: X.25, XODIAC

LAN Standards Supported

Proposed IEEE 802 Standard: yes
ISO Open Systems Interconnection Reference Model (OSI): yes; supports
  layers 1–5

LAN CHARACTERISTICS

UNGERMANN-BASS, INC.
NETWORK: NET/ONE

TYPE	DATA TYPE	TOPOLOGY
Network may be operated in broadband or baseband	Digital (baseband, broadband), audio (broadband), video (broadband)	Bus

SPECIFICATIONS

Operating Mode(s): half duplex

Access Method(s): CSMA/CD (baseband), CSMA (broadband)

Transmission Medium(s): coaxial cable

Data Transfer Rate(s): 10 Mbps (baseband); 5 Mbps per CATV channel (broadband);

Number of Stations Supported; unlimited

Compatible Vendor Devices: none

Maximum Distance Between Devices: 20 miles

Communications Protocol(s) Supported: asynchronous, bisynchronous, SDLC, HDLC

LAN Standards Supported

Proposed IEEE 802 Standard: yes

ISO Open Systems Interconnection Reference Model (OSI): yes; supports layers 1–5

LAN CHARACTERISTICS

SYTEK, INC.
NETWORK: LOCALNET

TYPE	DATA TYPE	TOPOLOGY
Broadband	Digital, Audio, Video	Tree

SPECIFICATIONS

Operating Mode(s): full duplex
Access Method(s): CSMA/CD
Transmission Medium(s): coaxial cable
Data Transfer Rate(s): 19.2 Kbps
Number of Stations Supported: 20,000
Compatible Vendor Devices: any RS-232 device
Maximum Distance Between Devices: 50 kilometers
Communications Protocol(s) Supported: X.25
LAN Standards Supported
Propsed IEEE 802 Standard: yes
ISO Open System Interconnection Reference Model (OSI): yes; supports layers 1-5

Appendix B

Life Cycle Cost Factors

I. MAJOR NONRECURRING EXPENSES
   A. Hardware
      1. Procurement Cycle
         - Requirement analysis review
         - Feasibility studies review
         - Functional and technical specifications
         - RFP
         - Contract negotiations
         - Testing and evaluation
      2. Cost of Hardware
         - Communication handlers
         - Disks
         - Network controllers
         - Terminals
         - Printers
         - Modems
         - Displays
         - Other peripherals
         - Interfaces
      3. Modification and Integration
         - Engineering
         - Installation
         - Check-out
         - Documentation

    4. Site Modification
        - Additional space
        - Additional power
        - Additional air
  B. Software
    1. Procurement Cycle
        - Requirement analysis review
        - Feasibility studies review
        - Functional and technical specifications
        - RFP
        - Installation
        - Testing and evaluation
        - Contract negotiations
    2. Cost of Software
        - Studies
        - Designs (functional and details)
        - Reviews
        - Development
        - Testing (unit and integration)
        - Documentation
        - Implementation
        - Computer time
        - Supplies
        - Consultation if needed
  C. Personnel Costs
    1. Recruitment (including relocation)
    2. Operations training
    3. Hardware and software maintenance training
    4. Overhead
    5. Additional space
II. MAJOR RECURRING EXPENSES
  A. Hardware and Software Maintenance
    1. Cost of maintenance contract (included in the hardware/software procurement(s))
    2. Nonscheduled maintenance
    3. Personnel
    4. Travel, per diem; training (periodic)
    5. Additional new equipment including rentals
    6. Additional modification(s)
  B. In-House Costs
    1. Personnel
    2. Utilities
    3. Materials and supplies

Appendix B

        4. Overhead
        5. Facilities
    C. Resource Sharing with Other Federal Government Agency(ies)
    D. Commercial Services Other Than Maintenance
        1. Time sharing
        2. Software license fees
III. COST OF MONEY
    A. Inflation Rate
    B. Government Discount
    C. Inflation/Discount Differential
    D. Residual Value

Appendix C

Redundant Equipment Reliability

Equipment redundancy has a number of negative aspects. Among these are the effect of a larger number of electrical connections, and the fact that unmanifested failure in equipment may be much harder to detect because the failure is masked by the very presence of redundant equipment. As an example, electrical connectors tend to deteriorate with age, creating a high resistant electrical path. These connectors may not become part of the operational unit until a switchover is required.

Switchover, if it is to be done quickly, requires complex equipment. One form of redundancy requires identical equipment to perform the same functions simultaneously, with the output being taken from the one that is operating correctly. Therefore, in addition to the two basic units, more equipment is required to tell when a unit is not operating properly, to switch automatically to the operating unit, and to provide a status indicator to some monitor. A second form of redundancy requires that the second unit start operating only after failure of the first. This method still requires the same amount of equipment as the first, but has the advantage of less power consumption.

There may also be a severe problem due to loss of data, requiring elaborate means in the data transmitting and receiving hosts to ensure safe retention of data during switchover. With adequate hardware and software protection, the switchover can be detected by a transmitting host or network interface unit and the lost data replaced by retransmission. A less sophisticated host would not recognize the loss of data and the receiving host would either abort or accept bad data unknowingly. With the use of microcomputers being more predominant, the latter situation would be more likely.

Appendix C

Standby status, switchover criteria, and timing, all increase with the complexity of using redundant equipment to improve reliability. The *Systems Engineering Handbook*, published by McGraw-Hill and edited by Robert E. Machol, has additional information concerning the realistic reliability of redundant equipment involving several types of configurations.

Appendix D

Data Errors

1.0 INTRODUCTION

It is inevitable that any data communications circuit which is used to link remotely located computers and terminals will make data errors. There are several causes of these errors and the presence of errors may or may not be detrimental to system performance. This paper will discuss some of the causes and effects of data errors and precautions which may be taken to minimize them.

2.0 CAUSES OF DATA ERRORS

The sources of data errors may be classified as internal and external. Those error sources which are internal to the data communications equipment may be minimized, but not totally eliminated, through careful design. External causes of error are induced into the system from the environment. The primary means of minimizing errors caused by the environment is protection of the system. The environment of a system includes the surroundings of the separate elements of the system, such as the media which link these elements. Some of the phenomena which lead to data errors are:

- Noise, both white and impulse
- Crosstalk
- Intermodulation noise

Appendix D

- Echoes
- Phase changes
- Harmonic distortion
- Delay distortion
- Bias and characteristic distortion

Detailed descriptions of these impediments to accurate communications may be found in many texts, including *Telecommunications and the Computer* by James Martin (Prentice-Hall, 1976). The amount of effort which has been placed on minimizing the effects of the problems mentioned is made apparent by the accuracy of the ensuing data communications.

3.0 EFFECT OF DATA ERRORS

This effect may be immaterial in many instances, such as when a person is sending character-oriented information to another terminal. The occasional presence of an incorrect character does not prevent delivery of the intended information. In the case of bit-oriented, packetized information, the protocols include methods of detecting bit errors. The usual response of a system to bit errors is to request retransmission of the erroneous packet or all packets that were sent from a specified time up to the erroneous packet. The retransmission of data in which errors have been detected makes possible the improvement of system performance by a factor of 10^2 to 10^3. However, retransmission also adds delay in the successful delivery of information. In a local network of computers a major service which is made available is the ability to use the network media for transferring data-base contents between users. In the event data errors are detected, some lower-level peripheral devices, such as floppy disk controllers, will reject the data and return program control to the processor. The operator must restart the data transfer when this takes place. These restarts are not only time consuming, but they are a major source of frustration to someone who is attempting to make use of the information in a computer file.

The impact of data errors is better illustrated by the assessment of the frequency with which errors may be expected to occur. The specified bit error rate of common PBX systems is 10^{-7}, or one error may be expected for every 10 million bits of data. At a data rate of 56Kbps, an average of 20 bit errors could occur per hour, as derived below:

$$56 \times 10^3 \times 60 = 3.36 \text{ million bits per minute}$$
$$3.36 \times 10^6 \times 60 = 201.6 \text{ million bits per hour}$$
$$201.6 \div 10^7 = 20.16 \text{ bit errors per hour.}$$

Therefore, even an error rate which does not sound too bad on the surface can be the source of dissatisfaction to the system end-user.

4.0 PROTECTION OF THE SYSTEM

The communications media in a local network often consist of cable of some type. The cable must be routed through various environments, some of which are likely to contain major interferers to data accuracy. In a large office building there are many fluorescent lights, and also there are large motors which drive air conditioning and heating systems. These and other devices which move large currents often cause transient pulses which can lead to data errors. There are two methods of protecting a system from these disturbances: filtering and shielding. Filtering involves internal system power supply design to minimize the conduction of unwanted transients. Shielding includes equipment enclosures and interconnecting cables.

This discussion is primarily concerned with cable shielding, as it is a matter of system design to assure adequate protection of circuitry. The most effective method of eliminating unwanted coupling is to isolate the disturbed circuit from the source of interference by some form of shielding. However, magnetic and electric coupling are affected by different types of shielding; therefore, it is recommended that shielding be tailored to a specific application. An effective system design should include testing to determine the nature of interference and to enable a specific means of protection to be implemented. Otherwise, the system end-user is likely to be less than satisfied.

Appendix E

Packet Transmission

The following charts illustrate the approach used in determining the probable number of packets within a packet window and the probable number of retransmissions required in a nonjamming environment. In a one-second interval there are 2500 terminals transmitting a total of 2350 packets and contending for 6500 packet windows. The probability of x packets attempting to use a packet window is expressed as

$$P(x) = \frac{m^x e^{-m}}{x!}$$

The mean number of packets per window for this Poisson distribution is

$$m = 2350/6500 = 0.362$$

x Number of packets in slot	e^{-m}	$\dfrac{m^x}{x!}$	P	Number of slots having x $N(x) = P(x) \times 6500$	Number of packets involved $P(x) \times 6500 \times (x)$	
0	0.6963	1.	0.6963	4526.	0.	⎱ Packets
1	0.6963	0.362	0.2521	1638.	1638.	⎰ trans-mitted
2	0.6963	0.0655	0.04561	296.	592.0	712
3	0.6963	0.00791	0.00551	35.75	107.2	to
4	0.6963	0.00072	0.00050	3.25	13.0	be
5	0.6963	0.000052	0.000036	0.234	1.17	retrans-
6	0.6963	0.000006	0.0000042	0.039	0.234	mitted
7	0.6963	0.00000025	0.000000174	0.001131	0.007	
•	•	•	•	•	•	
•	•	•	•	•	•	
•	•	•	•	•	•	
N	•	•	•	•	•	
				6500	2350	

712 packets to be retransmitted contending for 6500 - 1638 = 4862 packet windows.

With 712 packets contending for 4862 packet windows, M = 712/4862 = 0.1464.

x	e^{-m}	$\dfrac{m^x}{x!}$	$P(x) = \dfrac{m^x e^{-m}}{x!}$	$N(x) = P(x) \times 862$	Packets = $P(x) \times (x) \times 4862$
0	0.8638	1	0.8638	4199.92	0
1	0.8638	0.1464	0.1265	615.04	615.04

615 packets transmitted
712 − 615 = 98 collided and will be contending for 4862 − 615 = 4247 slots.
m = 98/4247 = 0.02308

| 0 | 0.9772 | 1 | 0.9772 | 4150 | 0 |
| 1 | 0.9772 | 0.02308 | 0.02204 | 94 | 94 |

94 packets transmitted
98 − 94 = 4 collided and will be contending for 4247 − 94 = 4153 slots.
m = 4/4153 = 0.00096

| 0 | 0.999 | 1 | 0.999 | 4139* | |
| 1 | 0.999 | 0.00096 | 0.0001 | 4 | |

*Does not exactly equal 4150 due to rounding.

Appendix E

WAITING TIME

The time that a packet spends waiting to be transmitted is conservatively estimated by using the following analytical formula.*

$$\text{Prob (waiting time, } T>t) = B\, e^{-[(1-B)\, t/\text{AVS}]}$$

In the formula:

AVS = average time to transmit packet (51.2 μ s), and

B = bus utilization factor, ratio of average total traffic on bus to capacity of bus (1/6.34).

The equation is of the form:

$$\text{Prob } (T>t) = ae^{-bt}$$

where a = 1/6.34 = 0.1577, and b = (1 − 1/6.34)/51.2 = 0.01645. Then,

$$\text{Prob } (T>+) = 0.1577\, e^{-.01645t}$$

This cumulative distribution function can be used to determine the mean or expected waiting time, E(t).

$$E(t) = t \text{ such that}$$

$$\int_t^\infty \text{Prob } (T>t)dt = 0.5$$

Substituting Prob (T>t)

$$\int_t^\infty (ae^{-bt})dt = (a/b)e^{-bt} = .5$$

$$-bt = \text{Log}_e(.5b/a)$$

Substituting for a and b

$$-0.01645t = -2.9535$$

The average waiting time = 179.5 microseconds.

---

* R. Van Slyke, W. Chou, and H. Frank, "Avoiding Simulation in Simulating Computer Communication Networks," paper presented at the American Federation Information Processing Societies (AFIPS) Conference, New York, June 4-8, 1973, published in *AFIPS Conference Proceedings*. vol. 42.

Index

A

Advanced services, 7
American Telephone and Telegraph Company, 68
ARPANET, 3

B

Bandwidth, 5, 69
Baseband network, 1, 2, 14, 22, 36, 46-49, 60, 62-63, 66-72
    cost analysis, 60, 62-63
    design layout, 46-49
    general description, 14-15
    reliability, 36
    weighted rating, 66-72
Benchmark design, 35, 85
Broadband network, 1, 2, 14-15, 22, 50-54, 62, 64-65, 66-72, 73-84
    conceptual design, 73-84
    cost analysis, 62, 64-65
    design layout, 50-54
    general description, 14-15
    weighted rating, 66-72
Broadcast topology, 7
Buffers, 9
Bus topology, 8, 11, 12

C

Cable access point (CAP), 48
Calendar management, 25
Centralized control, 12
Centralized file access, 7
Channel access, 12
Circuit switching, 5, 10
Coaxial cable, 10, 46
Collision, 11, 13, 81
Communications, 5-6
    bursty, 5-6
    computer-to-computer, 6
    terminal-to-computer, 6
    transaction-oriented, 6
Comparison of alternatives, 56-72
    cost analysis, 58-63
    evaluation criteria, 56-57
    life cycle cost factors, 57-58
Components, 72-76
Conceptual design, 2, 73-85
Connection, 7
    multipoint, 7
    point-to-point, 7
Connectivity, 69-70
Contention control, 11, 79
Contention techniques, 13

Index

Control network technical approach, 24
CSMA/CD, 13, 22, 53-54, 69
Custom developed services, 7

D

Design:
    layouts, 2
    tradeoffs, 6
Device interface, 43, 50
Digital:
    data transmission, 31
    devices, 29
Digital Equipment Corporation, 3
Digitized voice, 7
Distributed:
    control, 12
    data base management, 7
    polling, 12
    processing, 6, 7
Dual cable network, 15

E

Electronic mail, 5, 7, 25
Equipment requirements, 81-82
Error control, 37
Ethernet, 3, 4, 10, 77
Evaluation criteria, 22

F

Fiber optic cable, 16
File transfer, 6
Fixed weight, 22

G

Gateways, 29, 31
General data processing, 7
Growth, 37, 69
    capability, 69
    requirements, 37

H

Hardware maintenance, 40, 70
Hybrid network, 1, 2, 54-55, 62, 66-72
    cost analysis, 62, 66-67
    design layout, 54-55
    weighted rating, 66-72

I

Imagery, 33
Information storage and retrieval, 7
Institute of Electrical and Electronic Engineers (IEEE) 802 Technical Committee, 16, 18, 38, 77
Intel, 3
Interface, 6, 27, 28
    node, 6
    standards, 27, 28
International Standards Organization (ISO), 16-18
    Seven-Layer Architectural Model, 16-18
Interprocess messages, 6

L

Life cycle, 57-62, 71
    cost analysis, 58-62, 71
    cost factors, 57-58
Local area networks, 3, 4, 19, 20, 25-26, 73-85
    characteristics, 4, 19
    concept, 3
    conceptual design, 73-85
    functional requirements, 25-26
    physical requirements, 26
    supported equipment, 26
    technical approach, 19, 20

M

Maintenance, 40, 41, 70
    hardware, 40, 70
    software, 41
Mesh topology, 8, 11
Message:
    network, 22, 76-82
    switching, 10
    transmission mechanism, 9
Model approach, 1, 7
Multiplexing techniques, 13, 14
Multipoint connection, 7, 13

N

National Bureau of Standards, 16, 18, 38
Network:
    access, 48
    communications flow, 46, 49
    delay, 34-35
    design, 6, 7, 35, 74

Network (*cont.*)
    interface units (NIUs), 11, 19, 50–53, 81–82
    nodes, 6–7
    operations requirements, 5
    reliability, 36–37, 49, 54
    traffic, 31–37
Network administration, 38–41, 82–84
    control, 39, 82–84
    maintenance, 40–41
    monitoring, 38, 82–84
Network topologies, 3, 7–12
    bus, 8, 10–12
    mesh, 8, 11
    multipoint, 3
    point-to-point, 3, 5
    ring, 3, 7–10, 12
    star, 3, 8, 10
    tree, 11
Node failure, 36
Non-digital devices, 29

O

Office automation, 6

P

Packet switching, 3
Palo Alto Research Center, 3
PBX, 1, 2, 13, 22, 36, 42–46, 59–61, 64, 66–72
    cost analysis, 59–61
    design layout, 42–46
    general description, 13
    reliability, 36
    weighted rating, 64, 66–72
Peripheral devices, 5
Point-to-point collection, 7, 13
Polling techniques, 12
Proprietary networks, 7
Protocol architecture, 5

R

Redundancy, 36
Reliability, 36–37, 68
Resource sharing, 7
Response time, 35, 69
Ring topology, 3, 7–10, 12

S

Security, 31, 70–71

Single cable network, 15
Software maintenance, 41
Specialized networks, 5
Star topology, 3, 8, 10, 36
Store-and-forward processing, 7, 10
Switching capacity, 10

T

Teleconferencing, 7, 14
Terminal access point (TAP), 48
Terminal to computer communications, 6, 26
Token passing, 8, 11–13
Topology, 3, 7–12, 36
    broadcast, 7
    bus, 8, 10–12
    mesh, 8, 11
    multipoint, 7
    point-to-point, 7
    ring, 7–10, 12
    star, 3, 8, 10, 36
    tree, 11
Traffic, 2, 33, 34
Transmissions, 5, 6, 9, 13, 33
    long haul facilities, 6
    medium, 5, 13
    mechanisms, 9
    video data, 33
    voice, 33
Tree topology, 11
Twisted pair, 13, 36, 46

U

User resource network (URN), 19, 24

V

Video data transmission, 33
Voice transmission, 33

W

Wangnet, 15
Weighted:
    matrix methodology, 1, 56–57, 64–71
    rating comparison, 71–72
Word processing, 6, 25

X

Xerox Palo Alto Research Center, 3